BA'
THE BOMBERS

by
WILHELM JOHNEN

Chapter I

THE FIRST KILL BY NIGHT

On April 9th, 1940, at 5:15 a.m., German troops had invaded Denmark and Norway. Hitler wished to forestall the British and to safeguard his north flank. The Luftwaffe squadrons stationed in Denmark were ordered to cover the troop movements planned for the invasion of Norway. The British tried to disrupt this action by constant day-and-night air attacks.

Major Falk in Aalborg was in command of a fighter wing, flying the famous Messerschmitt 110. This fast manoeuvrable fighter, equipped with two Daimler-Benz engines, ruled the air as far as the English coast. In daylight operational flights squadrons of these destroyer planes had been successful in air battles over the Channel against fast British bombers—Wellingtons and Bristol Blenheims. But the British not only flew by day—they also attacked important military objectives in Denmark by night. The R.A.F. pilots in night flying over the North Sea already displayed a skill which forced the Luftwaffe leaders to take their activities seriously. How were they to counter these night attacks? As so often happened in World War II, the pilots themselves took the initiative. Major Falk selected his best men. On bright moonlight nights he proposed to send his "aces" into the air to shoot down British bombers caught in the searchlight beams. The crews had never yet flown by night, but Major Falk, with his ruthless energy,

BATTLING THE BOMBERS

refused to abandon his idea of switching his best pilots over to night flying.

One bright night, after a short period of training, Oberleutnant Streib and Leutnant Mölders were on the tarmac ready to take off. The "Fluko"* reported that several bombers were flying in singly from the North Sea. The whole fighter wing was thrilled by the operation of these two Me. 110's. Oberleutnant Streib was the first to reach the green starting lamp. He turned his aircraft into wind and warmed up his engines. Mölders followed suit. The engines roared. The leading machine streaked across the flarepath, was airborne just before reaching the red lights at the end of the field and disappeared into the darkness. Mölders followed a few seconds later. Everything seemed to have gone remarkably well. The aircraft gained height and flew towards the searchlight zone.

The mission was soon over. The Britishers had turned for home and were on their way back to the coast. Major Falk gave orders for the airfield lights to be switched on to help the two pilots find the runway. In the distance the peaceful monotonous drone of the engines could already be heard. They were on their way back! Carefully the two machines flattened out and made perfect landings near the green lamp.

Streib and Mölders were not over-impressed by their nocturnal exploit. They both gave short accounts of what had happened to their pals. Streib, who was later to be the "Father" of night fighting, considered the chances of shooting down enemy planes at night very remote on account of the bad visibility. The crews looked sour.

* "Fluko" was an Air Reporting Centre, the regional headquarters of the air-raid warning system.

BATTLING THE BOMBERS

Mölders was not so pessimistic. "I can account for Streib's bad visibility," he said, commenting upon his friend's report. "I had the same experience. But then I got the idea of climbing higher to 7,500—9,000—even 11,000 feet. Above 10,000 feet the dark veil grew lighter and suddenly disappeared like a wraith. A starry sky lay above me and visibility was quite fantastic. I had no difficulty in keeping my aircraft on an even keel, for the broad horizon gave me a magnificent bearing." Major Falk's face brightened. He slapped both the officers on the back and then took them to his own quarters to work out a report on the first night mission.

The crews of Falk's wing began intensive training in blind flying. At the outset they were half-hearted. They disliked being taken off day flying. Some of the men asked to be relieved because they did not feel up to the demands made by night flying. At this juncture the decisive order came from higher quarters: "Major Falk's wing is posted to Gütersloh for blind-flying training with a view to night flying." The die had been cast. In a few weeks the Me. pilots learned blind night flying on machines equipped for that purpose. There was as yet no radar. Detection of the enemy remained purely a matter of luck.

On the 20th and 22nd July this new branch of the Luftwaffe was given a powerful stimulus. On the 20th July a British bomber squadron flew over the Ruhr. So far the flak alone had shot down an occasional enemy bomber. Now for the first time the night fighters joined in the task of protecting the homeland. Loose cloud banks through which the moon cast its light on the earth lay at 6,000 feet. Oberleutnant Streib came out above the clouds and flew towards the flak zone. Bright searchlights threw their beams against the ragged clouds, crossing each other in search of the enemy. In this maze of searchlight beams Streib spotted

BATTLING THE BOMBERS

his quarry—an Armstrong-Whitley bomber. He was surprised by the sinister shadow in the dark night sky. At full speed he dived on his enemy. In his excitement the first attack was wide. He banked sharply and got on to the tail of the bomber. The dark shadow loomed ever larger in his sights. I must shoot now, he thought. A long burst hit the bomber's petrol tank and set it on fire. The aircraft exploded and went into a spin. This happened on the 20th July, 1940, at 02:15 hours; it was the first enemy to be shot down by a night fighter in World War II. It was the start of the relentless night battles between England and Germany.

Two days later, on the 22nd July, Streib shot down his second enemy, a Whitley V. On the 30th August came his third victory, and on the following night his fourth—both Vickers Wellingtons. Oberleutnant Streib's name appeared in the Wehrmacht communiqués. At the same time the crews of Hauptmann Radusch's squadron, Oberleutnants Ehle-Griese, Wandam-Fenzke and Feldwebel Gildner-Kollak, won their first night victories.

On the 30th September, 1940, the decision was taken to develop night fighting on a grand scale. That night Streib shot down three Wellingtons within forty minutes and for this achievement was awarded the Knight's Cross. Major Falk was given the job of building up a night-flying group and was appointed its first commodore. At this time he went on a recruiting campaign for night-fighting pilots and appeared at the Fighter School in München-Schleissheim where I had just qualified as a brand-new lieutenant. Major Falk was a genial and plausible speaker. I trusted him, and after due consideration I decided to become a night fighter.

On the 10th May, 1941, we night-fighter candidates arrived at Stuttgart-Echterdingen. A magnificent May night

BATTLING THE BOMBERS

lay over Swabia. The airfield was brilliantly illuminated and red lamps indicated all the obstacles. The landing and take-off runways were flanked by rows of lights. The red, green and white navigating lights of the training machines twinkled like fireflies in the night sky. It was peaceful in our quarters. Presumably all the crews were in the air. We were enjoying the warm spring night and thinking of our new profession when suddenly a powerful scream and a whistle rent the air. Something fell like a comet from 6,000 feet vertically earthwards. I caught my breath. A terrific crash and a bright explosion . . . the ammunition had exploded, thousands of gallons of petrol blazed and lit up the dark night. A good start, I thought. If it goes on like that we must keep our fingers crossed when it comes to our turn. In a somewhat depressed mood we fledglings retired to bed.

I was faced with my first night-flying solo. The ground staff had got my Me. 110, C9-IU, ready to take the air. My wireless operator, Gefreiter Risop, a Berliner, was already in the machine, checking his radio apparatus. He looked serene and was fully occupied checking his waves—fantastic the confidence he had in me! Had I been in his place my heart would have been racing like mad having to set out on a night flight with a beginner. But Risop was quite unmoved. A magnificent fellow, that student from Berlin. I climbed into the front seat and put on my parachute. Then I closed my eyes and felt in the dark for the switches, buttons, instruments and wheels. We had practised these movements hundreds of times a day. Sixty consecutive hand movements had to be made in the right order and with precision. Twenty instruments had constantly to be watched; ten green and red lamps flashed, giving the necessary signals. I pressed on the electric starter and started the engines. While they were warming up I put on my helmet with the head-

BATTLING THE BOMBERS

phones and checked the contact with Risop, who sat directly behind me at his radio apparatus. A swift engine test, a green light—and I was all set. To the left and right of me twinkled the small flarepath lights. The aircraft trembled and quivered as I gave her full throttle. My speed increased, rose from forty to fifty to sixty, to seventy miles an hour. Tail up, flaps in, full throttle. I was airborne. Now I had to rely on my machine and on my skill as a pilot.

The night was pitch black and the brightly-lit airfield was my only bearing. What would happen if the lights were suddenly turned off and I had nothing but my phosphorescent instruments gleaming spectrally on the instrument panel? Fortunately I was kept so busy that these thoughts soon vanished. After making a wide circuit round the field I did a gentle left-hand turn, ready to come in and land. More hand movements, eager watching of the instruments and, as I approached the ground at a crazy speed, a last flattening out and a touch-down. The landing was very harsh and bumpy, but I had completed my first solo at night. I knew that I still had a lot to learn before I overcame my inhibitions against night flying and achieved a sense of security. I should fly now every night and do my tactical training by day.

At last the period of training was over and my night-flying course finished. Childish ailments were a thing of the past, and with self-confidence my pals and I joined the operational squadrons in the West. Leutnants Redlich, van Campe and I had been posted to No. 1 Night Fighter Wing in Venlo. A new life began Night fighting was still very much in its infancy.

In the Venlo officers' mess we newcomers were welcomed by the veterans of the First Wing of No. 1 Night Fighter Group. We found a number of officers there comfortably installed in armchairs—men who in the past few months had

BATTLING THE BOMBERS

been godfathers to the Night Fighter Arm. First and foremost was their commanding officer, who had just been awarded the Knight's Cross for his seventh victory. Next came the squadron leaders, Oberleutnants Timming, Wandam and Griese, and Leutnants Frank, Loos and Knacke. We could not hear too much about the experiences of these men in their victorious combats. We sat there tense and excited, listening to their stories.

"England"—these veterans said—"is taking reprisals on the Ruhr for the so-called 'Coventrating'[1] attacks by the Luftwaffe. The R.A.F. grows stronger every day and the number of bombers taking part at night has increased. So far we know the four twin-engined bombers—Whitleys, Bristol Blenheims, Vickers Wellingtons and Handley-Page Hampdens. Eighty to a hundred aircraft set out on fine nights to bomb the German cities. Thanks to the radio listening posts and the reconnaissance planes, we know the approximate starting time of the bomber formations. The enemy constantly changes his run-in course; feint attacks are launched on different cities to flummox the night fighters. During the last attacks we've noticed that the Tommies tune in on our wave-lengths and in perfect German give false information to the night-fighter squadrons. We have to look out for this and from time to time change our frequencies. The most difficult feature of night fighting is to find the enemy. To begin with, we've no radar and only vague information as to his position.

"The only possibility then is the trapping of the enemy in the searchlight beams. For this purpose in front of the Ruhr we've created a barrage of night-fighter sectors which are covered by two waves. Each of these sectors is provided

---

[1] A reference to the extremely heavy type of bombing attack made on Coventry.

BATTLING THE BOMBERS

with sufficient searchlight batteries to catch the enemy bombers in their beams when the weather is fine. Previously we had to circle at combat height over the beacon and try to spot a bomber flying at approximately the same altitude as ourselves. When one of them is caught in the searchlights we attack at once We have to be careful not to overshoot the mark The bombers fly at 220 m.p.h.; we, on the other hand, can dive on them at between 280 and 310 m.p.h. Moreover, the Britisher is a sportsman but very tough. He sells his skin dearly, and as soon as he sees a night fighter he blazes away with everything he's got.

"Surprise, of course, is half the battle. But remember that in summer there's a strong northern light. So attack from the dark side unless you want to be shot down. You must always think: with each bomber, death and destruction fly over our cities. Protect your country, your women and children from death out of the skies. Put all your efforts into the defence of your country."

These words of initiation rang somewhat differently from those we had heard at flying school. The Adjutant spread out a big map on which the night-fighting sectors were marked and gave us a full explanation.

On the same day we were posted to our individual squadrons. Leutnants Redlich and van Campe remained in Venlo. I was sent to No. 3 Squadron at Schleswig. Redlich and van Campe accompanied me to my machine. "Well, Johnen, we shall soon see who brings down the first Tommy. You fellows in Schleswig or we in Venlo. Don't forget your rubber dinghy, otherwise you'll come to a sticky end in the drink. Good hunting, and see you soon." Those were their farewell words. Both of them were brought down in the first air battles over Holland. The Tommy was quicker and more experienced.

Chapter II

SCHLESWIG DAYS

I LANDED shortly before 19.00 hours on the 25th June, 1941, at Schleswig. Mild, briny sea-air greeted me as I opened my cockpit roof. The mess huts were low rambling buildings surrounded by tall protective walls to the north of the airfield. There was a total black-out, and shortly after my landing many of the flarepath lights were turned off. My new station was shrouded in the friendly darkness of a summer night. The ground staff had already been notified and after a short greeting rolled my aircraft away to a dispersal pen and began to get it ready for ops. My radio operator looked after our packs and I went to Headquarters. Among a group of pilots I discovered my future superior officer, Oberleutnant Fenzke.

"Leutnant Johnen reporting for duty to No. 3 Squadron," I said.

"How are you, young fellow?" said Fenzke, holding out his hand. "These are your fellow pilots, Leutnant Schmitz and Leutnant Bender. You'll take over Officer of the Day from 22.00 hours. Tomorrow you'll take a flip in your crate and practise a few night landings."

It was all very pleasant and I had time to observe my new home at close quarters. But hardly had I finished my meal in the mess than the sirens wailed. They sent a shiver down my spine. The engines of the aircraft in readiness had been started by the sergeant mechanic and were now warming up. I rushed to the ops room and found the crews sitting in the dark. In this way the eyes became accustomed to the darkness. Oberleutnant Fenzke spread out a map and gave the position of the Britishers. Twenty bombers were flying over the North Sea, making for the Schleswig coast. Probable objective—Kiel. I turned hot when I heard this. Had it already come to this? But I was not to fly and envied my comrades Schmitz and Bender, who were already in their gear complete with oxygen masks, dinghies, Mae Wests and parachutes.

"Well," said Schmitz to Oberfeldwebel Wegener, "there's something doing to-day." The N.C.O. pilot was a calm, calculating man who at that moment was probably thinking of his wife and children.

"Yes, mein Leutnant. If only we can find them. The chaps in Venlo are all right with their searchlights. But we have absolutely nothing here except our night binoculars. Do you think you'll even find a Tommy with that gadget? My wife laughed herself sick when I told her of our game of hide-and-seek in the night sky. In any case, up there, you're well out of trouble, she said."

The men had to laugh but suddenly fell silent as Oberleutnant Fenzke gave them their flying detail.

"First Wave: Leutnant Schmitz flies in Sector C over Westerland. Leutnant Bender in Sector 2 over Föhr. Feldwebel E. in the sector over Pellworm, Oberleutnant Fenzke over Heligoland and Oberfeldwebel Wegener in the sector Husum-Schleswig. Pursue the enemy as far as the target and on the return journey. Leutnant Johnen takes over duties." I was proud of this responsible task and started my job immediately. The machines were reported ready to take off. A quick check of the landing and danger lights. All set. I stuck close to the Intelligence Officer and listened to the positional reports from Hamburg. The first coastal boats at sea

BATTLING THE BOMBERS

reported the arrival of a bomber formation. Control gave orders to take off. The crews rushed out into the darkness. The black Me. 110's stood like ghosts at the edge of the field. The exhaust pipes were equipped with suppressors so that not even the glowing gases should be seen by the enemy. The radio operators checked their sets The fighters started at short-intervals, making a circuit of the field to test the engines, and then disappeared in the darkness to their respective sectors. I was in telephonic communication with the various sectors and the listening posts soon reported the arrival of their fighters. The Intelligence Officers of the individual sectors knew their crews and felt responsible for the fate of their own fighters. This included Leutnant Krause from the Husum sector:

"Fighter at 15,000 feet, over the beacon," reported Krause, taking the opportunity of wishing me good luck for future ops. Then silence. One could have heard a pin drop, it was so tense and silent in the ops room. Conversation was in whispers so that each report could be clearly heard. Heligoland Sector reported the first drone of engines. Well, the "old man" was in the right spot again. Only last week he had shot down a bomber in this area. Heligoland next gave accurate reports of the enemy; the British were flying at 9,000 feet at a fair speed towards the coast. Apparently they were in a shallow dive on the run-in so as to increase their speed.

Then Krause, too, reported the first contacts. Oberfeldwebel Wegener was now directed into the fray. The bomber stream seemed to be heading for Schleswig. If only it would . . . Wegener reported propeller slipstreams. Krause gave him constant positional reports. I slipped quickly out into the open air and listened for sounds in the sky. In the far distance there was a slight drone which

BATTLING THE BOMBERS

grew stronger every moment. So it's Schleswig, I thought, and slipped back to my post.

Krause had begun to scream like a maniac in the telephone: "Wegener reports contact with enemy flying toward Schleswig."

My heart nearly stood still with excitement. It was my first night at a night-fighter station and events were following thick and fast. Wegener reported "Drums, drums" which meant an attack, and soon all of us were outside.

We could clearly hear the fast-revving British engines, interrupted now and then by the peaceful drone of the Me. 110. Then the firing started. At about 6,000 feet, Wegener was firing with all his guns at one of the bombers. I could not see the machines but I could follow the path of the tracers across the sky. A few bursts and a long trail of fire. Hell! That must be it. The British machine was like a blazing torch, but at the same moment Wegener received a burst of enemy fire from another direction. The bombers were obviously still in formation and protecting each other. I could hardly think. Wegener was also on fire. Like a comet with a long tail, he streaked across the night sky. "Bale out. Wegener, bale out," I screamed, as though he could have heard me up there. The next moment the British plane exploded about five miles away on the ground. A gigantic column of flame and a deafening explosion, and it was all over. Well, I thought, both of them got it. We must hope that Wegener and his radio operator managed to bale out. The two fires lit up the night. We could feel that the British were becoming nervous. The former regular drone changed to a restless roar of full throttle and the formation broke up. The effect of the raid would in this way be diminished. A few bombs fell on Kiel. The aircraft were hampered by the

BATTLING THE BOMBERS

flak and jettisoned their bombs in the open country. In broken formation, they made for home.

Oberleutnant Fenzke was still on the alert. On the run-in he had been unlucky. In the meantime I had ordered the fire engine and the ambulance to drive as fast as they could to the place where Wegener had crashed. Suddenly a report came in from Fenzke. There was activity in his sector. The first return flights were reported. I tuned in to Fenzke's wavelength since the other fighters were already on their way back. At first only loud noises could be heard on the Heligoland wave. The Intelligence Officer reported single bombers flying back at 3,000 feet. Fenzke lost height and took up his position to the dark south in order to see the bombers against the bright north light. He reported his position at exactly 3,000 feet over the sea. Now there was an icy stillness on the air. The British must be over Heligoland. The ground station gave Fenzke warning of engine drones directly over the island. What followed I will let Oberleutnant Fenzke relate in his own words:

"I had already been flying two hours over the pond. I thought to myself: it's a good thing it's summer, there must be a few patrol boats down there. Night fighting here in winter will be a bloody business. Then on the radio I heard the British report their position. 'Direct flight over the island at 3,000 feet.' I dived and turned south. Away to the north the Northern Lights were flashing. We scanned the horizon I flew between 2,700 and 3,300 feet in order to have a better chance of spotting a Tommy. Above us, the starry night; below us, the dark sea. Our eyes returned time after time to the clear sky in the north. We could see nothing. Once more the ground station reported enemy aircraft over the island. Our eyes were staring out of our heads as we peered into the darkness. From time to time I

BATTLING THE BOMBERS

looked through my night glasses but I could see even less and the nose of my machine was so high that my sparker began to get the breeze up. At that moment he said, "There's something moving on the horizon. Course 320.' I looked and could see nothing, but automatically I took up the course he had given.

"Suddenly, directly above the horizon, against the bright Northern Lights, I spotted a dark shape. It grew larger and soon I could see the outlines of an aircraft. A fat body, and a high tail unit—a Wellington. My heart was in my mouth. I hoped he hadn't spotted me. I stalked him, drawing closer, still protected by the darkness from the south. I was about 200 yards away. The Britisher was flying calmly, suspecting nothing. I closed in to 100 yards and got ready to fire. Now I could clearly see his glowing red exhaust pipes against the dark sky. I got the enemy bomber's left wing in my sights, but at that precise moment he banked sharply to the left. He had probably spotted me. The Wellington offered itself broadside as a target and my bursts soused into its body. It exploded in the air and fell in a host of burning debris into the depths. I shuddered as I thought of the crew. Flaming pieces of the aircraft splashed in the water. A blood-red circle of fire swiftly sank in the sea and once more everything was dark. I circled once over the spot where it had crashed, gave my position and asked the ground station to notify the Air/Sea Rescue, although I was convinced that the crew were beyond help. But nothing should remain undone."

So much for Oberleutnant Fenzke's report. We were all very proud of the two victories by our wing but what had happened to Wegener? Later in the night, the rescue team returned. Wegener was dead. I could not sleep that night for my nerves were too much on edge.

CHAPTER III

OPERATIONAL FLIGHT

During my first fortnight with a front-line squadron I had plenty of opportunity to make friends with my fellow pilots and to learn about the activities of a night-fighter squadron. As soon as dusk fell we were at readiness. Various members of the flying and technical staff had to be available within five minutes. The officers ate together in their mess and then joined their crews in the ops room. A short roll-call was followed by the met. report. Numerous weather stations of Germany and the occupied countries had sent in their teleprinter reports. These were complemented by reports from countless reconnaissance pilots who had flown as far as the English coast.

The Squadron Intelligence Officer next gave the secret frequencies to be used in radio transmission and the recognition signals of the night-flying aircraft and the airfields. These signals changed every night to prevent the enemy recognising landmarks. The night-flying crews could plot their exact positions by beacons installed on each airfield. This was particularly important in the event of a radio breakdown. The signal flares used by the night fighters were designed particularly for the flak. Whenever a machine was shot at when flying over a big city or a flak-protected zone, the radio operator had to fire one of these signal flares. They were mostly triple flares of green, white, red, blue or yellow. The British had spotted this and carried whole cases of carefully assorted ammunition for the outward journey. As soon as the

BATTLING THE BOMBERS

first enemy crew saw the recognition signal fired it immediately reported to the Master of Ceremonies of the bomber stream who relayed the information at once to all the British crews on a predetermined wavelength. Sometimes the code had to be changed several times in the course of a night. The British Master of Ceremonies was the pulse of the bomber stream. He carried no bombs but special radar equipment, navigational aids, parachute flares—the so-called Christmas trees—and flare markers. If this pathfinder were shot down by a night fighter the reserve Master of Ceremonies replaced him at the head of the bomber stream.

The crews were briefed by the Squadron Commander according to their quarters. The pilots, both officers and N.C.O.s, usually swapped experiences with their comrades in blacked-out waiting rooms. Models of enemy aircraft were often projected on to the ceiling with the aid of a bright torch in order to familiarize the crews with the enemy types. This lightning recognition of different opponents was decisive for the first attack, since each enemy machine had its own strengths and weaknesses and, above all, a different defence armament. The most dangerous was the rear gunner, who sat with four heavy machine-guns in a Perspex compartment behind the tail unit, waiting for the attacking night fighter. These "tail-end Charlies" were usually chosen for their courage, for the job made the greatest demands on the nerves. The man sat for six to eight hours entirely alone in his narrow unarmoured cage, and had to be on the alert the whole time lest a German night fighter should suddenly bob up out of the darkness and try to destroy him first with a well-aimed burst. If he were hit the fate of his machine was usually sealed.

The British did not raid the German cities every night.

BATTLING THE BOMBERS

Their crews, too, needed periods of rest and the gaps also had to be filled. Some nights therefore were spent in watching and endless waiting. On these occasions the crews read, played chess, cards or table tennis. From midnight onwards most of them lay down in full flying gear on the bunks in the rest room waiting for dawn to get a real rest in their own camp beds. The daily routine began once the sun was high in the sky. After lunch, flying training was carried out in the fighter rooms: target recognition, shooting practice, formation and combat flying. In the late afternoon the entire squadron, from the Commander to the newest recruit, went in for sport of all kinds to keep fit after so much time spent sitting in the aircraft or on the ground. Thus the days slipped by and not until the sun sank in a blaze of red into the sea did the hour of the night fighters come.

And this was the case on the 11th July, 1941, when I set out on my first operational flight. By now I had complete confidence in my machine. I could perform all the necessary movements with the certainty of a sleep-walker. I could instinctively feel the slightest movement of the aircraft in the air. Our expert had prophesied bad weather. Black clouds hung in the sky and a stiff breeze was blowing off the sea. No attack was anticipated and the Squadron Commander had briefed the newest crews for the first wave. Peace reigned in the waiting rooms and the crews had already retired to lie down on their bunks. My sparker and I were still playing chess. From time to time we went outside and looked up at the sky. Not a star to be seen. Bright flashes of lightning to the west. The wind had increased in violence and we imagined that we could hear the sea breaking on the shore; this was pure imagination for we were too far away.

BATTLING THE BOMBERS

Unless we were very much mistaken we should have a magnificent thunderstorm within a couple of hours.

"Let's hope we don't have to do our first ops in this bloody weather," said my operator, pushing hard against the door to cope with the wind.

We lay down on our bunks and wondered what the wind speed would be up there at between 12,000 and 15,000 feet. Well, we were soon to find out.

"*Achtung, achtung!* Immediate readiness for Johnen and Schallek crews! Bombers flying singly reported over the North Sea."

I was on my feet in a flash and through the door on the way to my plane.

"Take it easy, Johnen," cried the Squadron Commander. "Don't forget your operator or your Mae West. Act swiftly and calmly—don't lose your head."

In actual fact I was very excited and had to force myself to be calm. There were still flashes of lightning in the western sky. The outlines of the machines gradually loomed up in the darkness. Black figures released the rudder-locking gear and stowed the parachutes aboard. Risop climbed into his seat and put on his headphones.

"Make for the Westerland sector. Enemy aircraft about 120 miles off the coast," droned the loudspeaker.

Well, we're off on our pleasure trip, I thought and taxied on to the flarepath. My machine slowly got under way and was speeding towards the last red danger lamp at the edge of the airfield. I pulled gently on the steering column and was swallowed up in the darkness. Everything that bound me to the earth had been erased and, with blind confidence in my good old Me. 110 and in the skill of my wireless operator, I set course for the Westerland sector. Only for

BATTLING THE BOMBERS

a brief second did I dare to look outside. Wisps of cloud passed by my wings and as far as I could see there was nothing but cloud and more cloud. My variometer showed a steady climb of 9 feet per second and the air speed indicator oscillated peacefully between 200 and 215 m.p.h. Since the phosphorus-coated instruments blinded me, I turned the small shaded lamps down to their weakest. Strong gusts of wind tossed the machine about and made flying difficult. The rain lashed against the armour plating and streamed down the cockpit hood in heavy drops. From time to time, when a flash of lightning lit up the darkness, I could distinguish a gigantic bank of clouds towering to 12,000 feet. The Westerland ground station was very faint.

"Argus 4 from Meteor Argus 4 from Meteor Come in please, come in please."

Risop gave our altitude and course. At that moment we must have been at 9,000 feet over the coast; we were still ploughing our way through the thick clouds and the wind became more and more gusty. Gradually our communication with the ground station grew clearer. The powerful head wind cut down our speed and we had needed almost double our normal flying time to reach our ground station on the island of Sylt. The minutes seemed an eternity and the ground station kept on calling to us, asking why we were lagging.

In the meantime the British, having the advantage of a tail wind, were at 13,500 feet almost off the coast. I got the best out of my machine, finally coming out of the cloud bank into a clear starry sky.

"Argus 4 from Meteor. Argus 4 from Meteor. Come in aircraft flying over Westerland on course 130. Altitude 13,500 feet."

I was now on the opposite course speeding directly

BATTLING THE BOMBERS

towards them a few feet above the clouds in order to spot the opponent either against the bright night sky or against the white cloud bank.

"Turn on to the enemy course 130," repeated the fighter controller. "You must be very near the enemy."

I swung immediately on to course 130. The engines were running smoothly, which gave me confidence; I had an exciting feeling that we were among the Tommies and I was very wide awake. Risop had already reported to the ground station and was peering through his glasses at the night sky. Suddenly I felt the first slipstream, which flung my machine about wildly. I reacted as quick as lightning and put on opposite rudder. More slipstreams. My machine banked and was on the point of going into a spin. We must have been flying directly behind the British. I gripped the stick tightly between my knees and put on my oxygen mask to shake off a slight feeling of weariness caused by the altitude. At the first few breaths bright coloured stars raced before my eyes but then my head was quite clear once more.

"There's one," shouted Risop, "right ahead and level with us." Instinctively my right thumb released the safety catch of my cannon and six red lamps flashed. The weapons were ready to fire, but the Tommy had disappeared. "He's broken away to starboard," cried Risop, looking through his glasses. I pushed the throttle full home but the darkness protected the enemy and swallowed him up. "If you hadn't loaded straight away he wouldn't have given us the slip," said Risop.

I had to admit that in the first excitement the cannon were my first consideration, for it is a consoling feeling to sit behind such powerful weapons. "Never mind, Risop," I said, "we'll soon find another one." Tirelessly we cruised round the sky, looking and looking, but the Tommies seemed to have been spirited away. Our eyes gradually began to hurt from staring into the darkness. Behind each star, behind each cloud, we suspected a Tommy.

"Well," said Risop dryly, "those vitamin pills to help us see don't seem to be much cop—not to mention those eternal raw swedes the quack makes us eat every evening." He tried to get in touch with the ground station once more. "We ought to have radar aboard," he grumbled.

And the hunt went on. Every moment we hoped to find one of the enemy, but we found nothing but clouds, stars and darkness. In the meantime our radio had fallen quite silent and our course was still 130.

"Where are we actually?" I asked Risop, trying to study the map by my dimmed torch.

"If only I knew, sir. It's as silent as the grave in my spark box."

According to our flying time we must have been in the neighbourhood of Schleswig. Well, we had plenty of fuel so I flew on blithely for some moments in the hope of still coming to grips with the enemy. It was all in vain, as I was to learn later. After flying over the coast the British had kept on the same course for about ten minutes and then turned sharply on to 180°, going down 5,000 feet and making for Hamburg. The ground station could no longer reach us when it received this report.

The hope of making our first kill evaporated in the storm. All our efforts were now concentrated on finding our position. Risop paid out the aerial and tried to get a bearing by a radio compass station for a ground to air reply was no longer possible. He continued to give our code number over the air. After a long wait the ground station at Schleswig finally replied, with our morse signal, but the reception was still so weak that the letters were drowned by disturbance. What next? Our last resort, to which we clung as to a straw, was our own fix. Risop went over to the wave of a heavy radio beacon near Schleswig whose call sign we got very weakly in the headphones. The bearing showed a new course of 70°.

"That can't be right, Risop," I said. "Our position on that course would be south-west of Schleswig."

"Well, if you think you can do any better, have a go," came the surly reply.

Another attempt at a fix gave the same course—70°. Since I found this ridiculous, I lost height in order to catch sight of the ground. The weather had improved but the wind was still blowing just as strongly. At 3,000 feet I came through the last cloud and saw below me something dark and grey. No light, no beacons, nothing but grey. Not a landmark. Without blind-flying instruments we should be hopelessly lost. Our predicament began to disturb me and even Risop was now not so sure of himself.

"My dear Risop," I said calmly, "either you get a proper bearing or before long we'll be splashing about somewhere in the water." There was a constant spluttering and crackling in Risop's receiving set until finally he got an intelligent bearing.

"New bearing 200," he said brightly.

That was almost the opposite direction. I breathed with relief and immediately changed on to the new course. We were now flying at 1,000 feet and below us we could see water as far as the eye could reach. The minutes seemed interminable but the ever stronger reception in our set allowed us to suppose that we were on the right course. My eyes bored into the night, looking for any small sign of light. The gale had carried us far out over the Baltic and now we struggled slowly against the wind on our way back to the coast. At last in the distance we saw the faint gleam of three searchlights pointing straight up into the sky. This sign meant that we had already been reported overdue and all ground stations were sending us the direction signals.

Well, I thought, where you find searchlights you must also find land. Slowly we approached the beams which, as we flew over, flashed on and off. We switched on our navigating lights and fired our recognition flares. Risop had recognized the searchlight battery as being east of Eckernforde. Now nothing could go wrong. Sweating profusely we touched down on our home field. My mates had long since landed and greeted us lost sheep with malicious laughter. "Did you intend to go fishing in the Baltic?" one of them asked my radio operator.

But Risop was ready with his repartee. "Well, if I'd had you on the end of a line as bait it would have been all right."

And so ended my first operational flight as a night fighter.

Chapter IV

TRIUMPH AND DISASTER

Through our intelligence service we learned of the R.A.F.'s gigantic preparations for the destruction of the German armament centres and large cities. The aim of this air offensive was obvious: Germany was to be beaten to pulp on the home front. In a long-term offensive which, according to Churchill's words, would cost England "blood, sweat and tears", the German key points and industry were to be sys-

BATTLING THE BOMBERS

tematically wiped out and a death blow dealt to the German cities and population. From now onwards the war was to be waged against women, children and civilians. The hatred among the nations now seemed to know no bounds. Belief in God and justice was shaken and mankind had become diabolical.

All over Great Britain huge airfields were built as take-off bases for the bomber squadrons. The aircraft industry worked day and night on the new four-engined bombers—Short Stirlings, Lancasters and Halifaxes—which could carry up to ten tons of bombs over Germany. The British Air Staff produced a comprehensive plan for a series of night attacks on the German cities worked out to the day, the hour and the minute.

But our defence was not asleep. New night-fighter wings came into being overnight. A barrage of night-fighter and flak sectors stretched from France across Belgium, Holland and Germany, right up to Denmark. Our Schleswig base was one link of this long chain.

After twenty-nine night missions I was an old hand at the game. I had grown to be part and parcel of my machine and night after night my self-confidence increased. So far those who had been shot down were mainly young inexperienced night fighters who had been too busy flying their machines. Luckily for me my first twenty-nine missions were completed without any contact with the enemy. Nor had my squadron had very much success apart from a few day and night victories. We lived a carefree existence during the day, enjoying this respite, until one grey November day in 1941 our C.O., Hauptmann Streib, appeared in ops room after a fine blind landing and told us that the squadron had been posted to Venlo.

This news was a pleasant surprise for me for Venlo was

not far away from my home town of Homberg. The ground staff and the girls of Schleswig, however, were not so pleased, and there were quite a few tears at our departure. In a low flight over the town, No. 3 Squadron of No. I Night-Fighter Wing said farewell to their airfield. Venlo lies on the Dutch-German frontier not far from the Ruhr. The Dutch population was correct but anti-German and as a result we rarely left our base. At Christmas, 1941, I went on leave to Homberg. The morale of the people was good despite the constant air raid warnings and the perpetual blackout. Everyone believed sincerely in final victory. Thanks to the heavy ground defences, destruction in the Ruhr had been insignificant. So far night fighters had not been used over the Ruhr because of the danger of being shot down by their own flak. The civilians pitied the British bomber crews who were shot down. How could the R.A.F. send their boys so irresponsibly to their certain death? Everyone hoped that peace would not be long delayed for one special announcement followed the other.

On the 26th March, 1942, at 20.00 hours in the briefing room of our night-fighter group at Venlo, we listened to the met. Then the C.O. gave the wave detail for the night. We had forty aircraft at Venlo. The wing was fully aware of its tradition as the first night-fighter wing in Germany. Many victories in the air had already been won and the C.O. himself had the highest score. It is not surprising that he was admired by all the men under his command. The crews were close pressed in the ops room, listening to the final briefing.

"The listening posts on the channel coast have announced the preparation of a large raid by the British bomber formations. The weather is favourable to the defence. Presumably the enemy will choose the Ruhr as the nearest objective in order to avoid unnecessary losses. After the first wave is airborne the second will be in immediate readiness. The third wave remains in a state of alert. We are flying over the Ruhr today for the first time. The flak has been notified and will limit its fire to 15,000 feet. The searchlight beams above 15,000 feet will be our arena. It is essential to observe a minimum altitude of 15,000 feet for the flak cannot guarantee the safety of the night-fighter aircraft below this."

There was a buzz among the crews: "Well, let's hope we're lucky."

"Should the flak fire above 15,000 feet despite their orders," the C.O. went on, "the night fighters concerned will fire distress and recognition flares. Incidentally, we are in constant telephonic communication with the Flak Divisional Commander on the Wolfsburg in Duisburg. The crews for the Ruhr mission will be notified later."

The crews did not look too happy at this news. The witches' cauldron over the Ruhr was well known—an unbroken sea of searchlights with thousands of flak guns! When all their guns were in action, even we pitied the poor Tommies who had to fly their heavy, unwieldly crates through this fiery holocaust. The British crews frequently jettisoned their bombs before reaching the objective and turned for home. And now we were to fight over this inferno of flak bursts. Even if the gunners observed their limit of 15,000 feet. . . . In this respect we had very little confidence in the gunners.

And now the Officer of the Day gave the final briefing: "Operation Ruhr. First wave Leutnant Johnen, second wave Feldwebel Lauer. The crews are to get in touch immediately with the Flak Liaison Officer and discuss with him the tactics of the operation. Until the alert signal is given the film *Quax, the crash pilot* will be shown in the mess together with German weekly newsreel."

Obviously they were trying to take our minds off things and this was all to the good, for no one felt particularly happy. My faithful radio operator, Risop, in the best of form as usual, fetched his navigation briefcase and spread the map out before me. Feldwebel Lauer's crew joined us. We were completely indifferent to Quax, the crash pilot, and it seemed more intelligent to work out our tactical preparations.

In a few brief words, the Flak Liaison Officer gave us the outlines of the operation. We had to fly from Venlo on a north-easterly course over a beacon near Wesel. This beacon would give the intermittent sign A F and report our arrival to the Wolfsburg. Our combat altitude of 17,000 feet had to be reached above this beacon. From this position we were to change over to a certain signal and be led by the flak apparatus over the target. In this way, the flak on each side of our position would recognise us and be able to get a bomber in the searchlights for us to shoot down. The flak would cease firing as soon as we were engaged.

"Good. In theory that's all very simple and clear, but in the heat of a scrap . . ." I replied to my mates of the ground defence.

Risop advised me to see that my parachute fitted well. Parachutes, in actual fact, were often exchanged or newly packed without anyone paying much attention to the size. And yet how important it was for the belt to fit close to the body! At a baling out speed of over 300 m.p.h., the opening jerk of the parachute brought into play great stresses which could have disastrous results if the belt were loose. Above all, the belly was in great danger in the case of loose thigh straps and many a pilot had cause to regret his irresponsibility in this respect. Our old parachute sergeant, Frobose, was soon on the spot and saw that our belts fitted.

"Is something special on, Herr Leutnant?" he asked genially, as he gave a final look at my "life-belt".

"No, Frobose—we only want to avoid being despatched into the next world."

Frobose gave a knowing laugh. "Well, good hunting," he said, "and if the parachute doesn't open when you bale out then come and get a new one from me tomorrow morning."

Once our preparations were finished we felt in the right mood to be cheered up by the antics of Quax, the pilot who committed all the faults in the calendar. There was great excitement in the theatre. The crews sat there smoking at their ease in the mess armchairs and did not spare their comments. The fighter controller, Oberleutnant Hittgen, was their special butt. We were all bent double with laughing and had soon forgotten our Ruhr operation as we enjoyed the misfortunes of poor Quax on the screen.

In the middle of the film the Officer of the Day put his head through the door and gave the order: "First Wave at readiness."

Quax was immediately turned off and the crews got into the bus which was to take them over to their machines. Heaven be praised, in Venlo we needed no Mae Wests or dinghies. The Chief Mechanic told me that my crate, Fritz Ludwig, was airworthy and helped me fasten my parachute. The engines were ready for a cold start. That meant one had to be particularly careful. A certain amount of petrol is mixed with crude oil causing considerable lubrication when the engines started and thus doing away with the need for warming up. But an immediate take off was necessary, for after five minutes the petrol evaporated from the actual heat of the engines. Then came the critical moment when the oil had not yet reached sufficiently high temperature, and the petrol had already evaporated. This critical moment must not be allowed to occur at the greatest moment of engine strain and therefore, above all, not at the start, because as a result of insufficient lubrication the pistons would become worn and the machine would inevitably be a write-off. Watching your instruments on a cold start is particularly important. At normal running speed, that is at cruising speed, the critical moment does not damage the engine. Risop and I were all set to take off and had put on our oxygen masks in readiness for our 17,000 feet ceiling. Above 13,000 feet on a steep climb a man can no longer live without oxygen and from this altitude the physical reactions and quick thinking are impaired. At a height of 17,000 feet two minutes without oxygen means certain death.

We had already put on our masks for the simple reason that putting them on in the air is always troublesome. Now we had plenty of time to make our preparations. My comrades were also sitting in their machines and occasionally I saw the flash of a torch, overhead a magnificent starry sky . . . Papa Hittgen in his role as fighter controller broadcast a lesson in astronomy with a pithy commentary. He knew how to keep the crews in a good mood and to banish the nervous tension of waiting. Even after the orders to take off had been given he would say farewell to the crews with the record: "Come back—I'm waiting for you." That night he had to wait a long time for me. As my pals told me later, he never gave up hope that I should return and did everything in his power to help me find the airfield until finally he learned that I had been shot down. All his arts were then, of course, in vain.

BATTLING THE BOMBERS

The Britishers were taking their time. The hand of my instrument panel clock stood at 21.30 hours. I suddenly felt like telephoning to my parents. Venlo was in direct communication with Duisburg and from there I could easily get the connection. This was, of course, strictly forbidden, but at this decisive moment I did not want to miss the opportunity. I sprang out of my aircraft and ran to the H.Q. truck.

Papa Hittgen, who from this point was in control of operations, looked dumbfounded when he saw me turn up. "Have you gone off your nut, Johnen?" he demanded. "Suppose the C.O. finds out? What are you doing here? Have you got stage fright or something? Doctor Siecke," he called out to the station quack, who was also in readiness. "Give Johnen a bromide."

I let him go on talking and already had the Wolfsburg on the line. There was a crackle in the receiver. My parents answered. Hittgen stared at me as though I had fallen out of the clouds, but before he could open his mouth, I was running back to my machine. The clock hand showed 21.45 hours when Hittgen despatched the first wave for the ops over Holland. The British bomber stream had assembled east of London over the Thames Estuary and was now flying on a direct course for the Ruhr.

Position of the bomber stream—west of Flushing on Walcheren. My comrades took off at short intervals. Each time the engines roared, a trail of sparks rained down on the flare path. The dark shadows swiftly disappeared on the horizon and set course for their beacons. 21.55 hours: at a great height I could hear the singing drone of a fast English machine. Presumably it was the pathfinder. In the distance I could hear the sirens wailing. 22.00 hours: still no orders for me to take off. I gradually grew both impatient and

BATTLING THE BOMBERS

nervous. Finally, at 22.02 hours: "Leutnant Johnen take-off." The inertia starters roared, the blades turned clumsily and soon both engines were running. "Good hunting," my mechanic shouted into the cockpit as he closed the roof. I pushed the speed lock forward and taxied to the starting point. 22.03 hours—airborne.

A bare twenty minutes later I reached the scheduled height of 17,000 feet and circled above my beacon west of Wesel. The sky towered majestically above me and the stars seemed to be closer, so wonderfully bright was the night. It was a serene and peaceful sight at this high altitude. Up there man feels the vastness of the cosmos and his own insignificance. The earth was far away. My fellow men down there were far away and yet it was my duty to preserve them from direct catastrophe. How dark it was below. Here and there I could see the blood red glow of the blast furnaces which, now that the enemy was approaching, would be extinguished. A few searchlights suddenly went on and began their play in the sky as though trying to warn the approaching bombers. Lights went on only to go out immediately. Even at that altitude I could feel the nervous haste of the men below in face of the threatening disaster. From south to north in a broad sweep glittered a smooth grey ribbon—the Rhine. The first landmark for the British. The earth seemed to have sunk into itself before the deadly danger from the air as though it would soon give a mighty scream of fear and despair at its tormentors. The first flares fell and flooded the landscape with a ghostly light. The British were looking for their target.

And now fell the parachute flares which opened at 1,500 feet and swayed slowly down to the ground. A hurricane burst upon the Tommies. Hundreds of searchlights went

BATTLING THE BOMBERS

on, pointing their thin fingers at the enemy bombers. Thousands of flak salvoes flashed, forming a box barrage round the Ruhr. The British Master of Ceremonies, however, proceeded imperturbably on his way, dropping his markers, the so-called "Christmas-trees". The parachute flares were still hanging like bunches of grapes over the landscape. According to my observations, Duisburg was probably being attacked. The ground station reported my pals' first successes over Holland. Two victories for my C.O., Hauptmann Streib, within eight minutes. In the meantime the Master of Ceremonies had found his target. He strewed the sky with red, green, and white flares which really looked like Christmas trees and with their harsh lights illuminated the objective—the harbour installations of Duisburg-Ruhrort.

His work was done and now hell was let loose. The flak kept up a continuous drum-fire on the approaching bombers. The shells burst and crackled between 1,200 and 1,500 feet. The Tommies were flying in fan formation, at graded heights, in order to divert the defence. Pitilessly the leading enemy machines were caught in the searchlight beams. Their silver bodies glittered like bright fishes against the dark night sky. The flak would not let its prey out of its claws. The fate of the bomber was sealed. In a matter of seconds, flight direction, speed and altitude were worked out on the flak gunners' instruments and, hit by the next salvo, the bomber crashed with its load into the depths. Three, four and five British machines were burning in the air. And they fell like comets earthwards.

I was completely engrossed by this grandiose performance and was really startled when the ground station suddenly called: "Buzzard 10 from Eagle. Give your fighter recognition signal. Course 130. Keep your prescribed al-

BATTLING THE BOMBERS

titude. Eighty enemy aircraft over Duisburg. We're handing you over to Wolfsburg. Message ended. That's all."

I checked my engines and navigating lights. Everything in order. Risop called up Wolfsburg: "Wolfsburg from Buzzard 10. Come in, please." The fighter controller reported immediately and gave me orders to attack any machine caught in the searchlight beams above 15,000 feet. I set my course straight for the witches' cauldron. The nearer I approached target, the brighter it grew around me. A sea of light from the bright searchlights blinded me, each time I made the slightest attempt to look down below. The flak shells crumped, some of them far above me, and I felt that I was now flying through Hell. The first explosion made my machine quiver as a shell burst fifty yards ahead of me. The next moment the blast seized my Me. 110 as with a giant's fist, and shook it.

"Get busy, Risop," I shouted. "Fire the recognition signals. The next one will get us." But already two green and one white flare had burst in the sky.

"Are those bloody idiots trying to shoot us down?" roared Risop reloading his flare pistol.

Instinctively I had put the machine into a steep left-hand turn. The next salvo burst behind us. We're not going to make it as easy for you as that, I thought. Ahead of me a cluster of searchlights were lighting up the sky. Hesitantly the white beams flitted to and fro like the arms of an octopus until at last they had caught a bomber. The British machine was flying at about 14,500 feet and took no avoiding action. The gunners below made him their target but they were shooting too far ahead. I decided to attack. Risop quickly transmitted the code word: *"Pauke, Pauke"* to the ground station. I dived from my superior altitude and got the bomber in my sights. The air speed indicator needle rose

BATTLING THE BOMBERS

to 330 m.p.h. The bomber grew ever larger in the sights. Now I could clearly see the tall tail unit and the rear gunner's Perspex turret. My machine came into the searchlight area and a few well-aimed bursts lashed the bomber's fuselage, tearing off huge pieces of the fabric. The Tommy was on fire and turned over on its back. Everything happened in a flash. At incredible speed I streaked past the burning British bomber and zoomed high into the sky to escape the threatening flak bursts.

"Good stuff, Herr Leutnant. Good stuff," shouted Risop and reported our first victory to the ground station: "Wolfsburg from Buzzard 10. A Vickers Wellington shot down. Congratulations, Herr Leutnant, carry on the good work and perhaps we'll get another."

A swift glance below. The Tommy had hit the deck and exploded. Fires had been caused among the harbour installations and were glowing scarlet in the glare of the searchlights. The other Britishers had seen their comrade go down in flames and lost their nerve in the fiery tempest over Duisburg. They dropped their bombs at random all over the city. The ground station reported the first return flights.

Risop suddenly called out: "There's one above us."

I could only vaguely recognise the outlines of an enemy aircraft. What a miracle! We had spotted him without a searchlight, without radar and without direction. The bomber was flying at a fairly high speed on a northerly course. My nerves were on edge. I forced myself to be calm and pulled up my nose. Slowly the monster drew closer—to forty, thirty, twenty yards. We must have looked very small and insignificant compared with this mighty "barn door" with its gigantic wings covering the sky.

BATTLING THE BOMBERS

"It's a four-engine," stammered Risop. "We haven't seen this type before."

I was now flying close below the bomber and took a breather. The enemy machine continued north-west on its homeward course, presumably quite unaware of the pursuer below. But I made a great mistake. The Tommy had long since spotted me. This was the first time that the Short Stirling four-engined bomber, carrying a ten ton load, had appeared in the Ruhr zone. Our defence knew nothing of this type. Risop and I were therefore unaware that beneath the fuselage sat a gunner with two heavy machine-guns to protect this weak spot.

In blissful ignorance we continued to fly below him, watching the glowing exhaust pipes of the four radial engines.

"How shall we attack?" asked Risop.

I thought for a second and decided that the best method would be from below in order to let the bomber pass across my sights and then to give him a good burst in the fuselage. The most dangerous moment would be when I zoomed behind his tail and the propeller slipstream of his engines caught my aircraft. I therefore had to aim vertically at his fuselage in order to put "Tail-end Charlie" out of action.

"It's time to fire," said Risop. "Otherwise he'll spot us. Put your trust in God and wade in, Herr Leutnant." Those were his last words.

I throttled back, let the bomber forge ahead and put on top rudder. The protruding nose appeared in my sights. At the same moment our bursts crossed. As out of a watering can, the enemy's tracers bore down on me from all the guns, completely blinding me. My aircraft was caught in the slipstream and tossed about like a scrap of paper. It was impossible to aim. The broadside of my Me. 110 afforded the

BATTLING THE BOMBERS

Stirling gunner an excellent target and the bullets lashed my cockpit, fuselage and petrol tanks. In a fraction of a second my machine was transformed into a flaming torch. Scores of gallons of petrol were alight, the flames were already licking the cockpit. A machine-gun salvo grazed my left leg and tore away the bundle of recognition flares attached to my left calf. The cockpit roof was torn off by the weight of the explosion and flew away. At this moment of almost certain death, I cast a glance at Risop. He had slumped forward, lifeless, over his radio. The machine gun bursts had killed him. My hope of getting out of the burning machine as it fell vertically into the yawning depths was very slight. The appalling heat in this sea of flames almost made me lose consciousness.

I felt no fear. With a desperate effort, I hoisted my wounded leg out of the cockpit, but centrifugal force was too strong and forced me back into the aircraft. So I abandoned all hope of being saved and put my hands up to shield my eyes. After a dive of 9,000 feet the aircraft exploded in the air and flung me out. As a burning torch I hurtled through the air on my back. The cool night air lashed my face and revived me. Like a flash the thought ran through my head: the parachute is on fire. The silk cords were still in the pack protected from the greedy flames. I quickly put out the flames with both hands and tore off my flying boots and gloves. I got away with it. It was high time to open the parachute for the red fires below seemed to be approaching at a terrifying speed. The earth drew closer and closer. A sudden jerk stopped my breathtaking fall. The parachute opened. My joy was undescribable but it was soon to be dampened: the parachute was torn and had bullet holes in it. My nerves were at breaking point. And yet somehow I pulled myself together. I was now terribly afraid. During the dive I had hardly had time to realise things for they went too fast. But now in this leisurely descent I saw myself lying at any moment with broken limbs on some street pavement. And yet the earth did not seem to draw any nearer. One of the sixteen lines was shot through and was fluttering in the wind. The parachute was on a slant in the air and threatened at any minute to roman candle. That would have been the end. With my last strength I tugged on the opposite lift webs and righted the canopy. During this last desperate action I crashed heavily into the water of a flooded meadow and sank up to the neck in the mud. Again my luck held. The bad effects of my clumsy landing were offset by the soft soil. The cold water completely revived me. I fired my revolver into the air for someone to come and rescue me. Some men hurried up and freed me from my tricky situation. Then I fainted. When, after some hours, I opened my eyes a sister was bending over me with a smile. I was saved.

Chapter V

RECOVERY

The worst was over. The head doctor of the hospital allowed me to take my first walk along the corridors. Supported by the sister, I looked out on to the gardens; the blossoms on the trees and the bright flowers of spring gave me a new urge to live. Only the thought of my trusty radio operator Risop cast a shadow on my joy. The C.O told me that they had had great difficulty in recovering Risop's body. The nose of the machine as it hit the ground

BATTLING THE BOMBERS

like a torpedo had bored deep into the marshy ground and taken Risop down with it into the depths.

The sister described what had happened since I had been brought into hospital: "You worried us, Herr Leutnant. At 1.30 in the morning the telephone rang in my ward. A night fighter had been shot down and the pilot lay unconscious and badly wounded in a peasant house. You were soon brought here and our chief surgeon took you under his wing. Now we've patched you up but you won't be able to fly again. Your eyes have suffered too much from the heat. Not until the burnt skin peeled from your face did the swelling go down. The doctor could then lift your eyelids and examine the skin below. One of the sisters wept for joy when he said that you would be able to see again."

The sister's words aroused my deepest gratitude. After removing a host of splinters, the doctor managed to save my left leg and I was able to walk again after two months. Despite second degree burns, there was no trace of a scar on my face. Although I suffered a great deal of pain, my health improved day by day and the new skin gradually replaced the old.

Now I was climbing up towards life again and enjoying my convalescence. My thoughts turned to my squadron at Venlo, and to my comrades. Should I ever be able to fly again? The sister's words became a nightmare. At last I was discharged. My limbs still aching and with a new face, I set out on my leave for Bad Schachen.

Our Group M.O., Dr. Siecke, examined my eyes and smiled. "You've had a great stroke of luck, my dear Johnen," he said. "You'll be able to fly again in a fortnight. But don't get spotted a second time, because you might not get out of it so well."

BATTLING THE BOMBERS

My squadron commander gave me a new radio operator, Obergefreiter Ostreicher, a typical easy-going Viennese who was never ruffled. "Well, what do you know, Herr Leutnant?" he kept saying as we studied the fatal Short Stirling.

Every evening I sat with the young crews, working out the best methods of attacking this new type of bomber. By day I flew my new operational machine "Dora" to get accustomed to her. My inhibitions soon vanished and I recovered my confidence in the machine.

One warm summer evening in July, 1942, the C.O., after a conference with the Station M.O., put me on ops as reserve in Berta Sector. The fighter controller of this region, Oberleutnant Knickmeier, telephoned and wished me good luck on my first op since the accident. My position in reserve gave me little hope of having a brisk encounter and I had no expectations of meeting a Tommy that night.

I was therefore slightly surprised when my Viennese radio operator stumbled into my hut with the words: "Herr Leutnant, get ready. The enemy's on the way. The boys are already airborne."

"Okay," I replied, imitating his Viennese accent. "We'd better get a move on."

I got dressed with quiet deliberation and made my necessary preparations. The raiders flew fairly high over our airfield in the direction of the Ruhr, dropping a few bombs on our installations by way of greeting. The fire engine was on the spot and a few insignificant fires were soon under control.

The ops room was in an uproar. Various lines were engaged and each time the shooting down of a bomber was reported there was a loud cheer. The C.O. was flying in Sector Berta, which lay nearest to our airfield; this sector

BATTLING THE BOMBERS

had the greatest number of penetrations recorded, a magnificent fighter controller, and the most bombers shot down. This was once more the case that night. The "old man", after his second victory, reported heavy damage to his wings and engine. His Adjutant, Oberleutnant Frank, took off immediately to relieve him. But the raiders had gone and Frank had to wait for an hour over Berta for their return flight. This period of waiting was always very boring. Radio silence was imposed because the wireless operator had to be prepared to receive orders from below at any minute. Our Adjutant was at last relieved from the monotony by the first return flights and emulating his superior shot down a further two bombers. In the meantime Ostreicher and I, as reserves in "Dora", received orders to take off and engage the tail of the returning raiders should Oberleutnant Frank be put out of action. This precaution proved to be a wise one, for Frank had to make a landing owing to a damaged radio. Well, we're off again, I thought, as I climbed to 12,000 feet and this time without flak.

The nights are particularly bright in July. The Northern Lights proved fateful to the British. Out of eighty enemy bombers, thirty were brought down.

"Buzzard 10 from Berta. Enemy aircraft at 12,000 feet. Course 280. Fly on course 100. Two couriers[1] are entering your sector." This was my message from Oberleutnant Knickmeier. I had a strange feeling as I heard these words; they reminded me of the night of March 26th over Duisburg.

"Buzzard 10 from Berta. Bank to port on course 280. Courier at your altitude. Give her full throttle."

My thoughts quickly vanished at this call over the air

---

[1] "Courier" was the German Airforce expression for any enemy aircraft.

and the exciting search for the quarry began. They must be a few stragglers which had either been hit or were trying to catch up their comrades. At that moment Knickmeier called me again and ordered me to slow down. I had already overshot the British machines. I throttled back and lowered the flaps to brake my speed.

"Enemy aircraft at 12,000 feet on the same course, one mile to stern. Fly at 200 m.p.h. and keep your eyes open."

Almost at stalling speed I let the adversary approach, keeping my eyes on the bright horizon to the north. At last I saw a small shadow ahead. I dived immediately and got below him. This time I was not going to let him spot me. Surprise is half the battle. Once I had sighted the enemy I felt quite calm. I was in no hurry and I crept in closer and closer. The enemy bomber—a Vickers Wellington, was trundling wearily homewards. Knickmeier reported that the second bomber was flying further to the north out of my sector.

My operator chimed in at this moment: "Herr Leutnant. Fire into his wings. I'm sorry for those poor fellows."

I had little sympathy with them when I thought of my earlier experience, and aimed the cross of my sights on the enemy's port engine. The distance decreased—150 . . . 100 . . . 50 yards. The rear gunner had already fired a few bursts, but he could not aim properly because his pilot was taking avoiding action. The tracers flew across the sky like a necklace of broken beads. I stuck close on his tail and waited for a favourable moment.

Now the bomber's wings were spread out against the northern sky as he went into a left-hand turn. At this moment I levelled my aircraft and let him fly into the cross-wires of my sights. The left aileron appeared. I gave him a burst and his port engine was on fire. I had hit him and

BATTLING THE BOMBERS

was waiting for the crew to bale out. But nothing happened. The fire appeared to have gone out. The pilot had probably cut out his port engine and was trying to get away on one. I must make another attack then. I had to lower my wing flaps to keep at his speed. The Britisher seemed to be a wily old fox and tried to shake me off by stalling. Now, I was hanging like a limp feather in the sky. Each of us was trying to fly even slower.

I grew impatient and rashly attacked direct from the rear. The rear gunner was waiting for me to approach and as we drew closer my two cannon and four M.G.s were pointed at his heavy M.G.s. We opened fire at the same moment and as the burning bomber dived earthwards I noticed that my own plane had been hit. There was a smell of burning in the cockpit but I could not see any flames. Suddenly my elevator jammed and I dived steeply. It was a nasty situation. I let fly a juicy oath and my Viennese must have taken this as an alarm signal for when, after a 3,000 foot dive, my stick functioned once more and I had the machine in control a current of air blew through the cockpit. I looked behind but my radio operator had baled out and his seat was empty. This was no great surprise. He had apparently found our dive a bit too hot and baled out, on the principle that it was better to be alive hanging on a parachute than dead in the machine. Now that I had no radio any further combat was out of the question. Without radio bearings or positional reports from the ground I had to rely on my own instinct to bring my "Dora" safely home. My only hope was Knickmeier. He would probably have noticed that something was wrong and notify the surrounding airfields. After a quarter of an hour's flight between the Rhine and the Maas I saw flares—radishes as we called them—being fired in the distance. In the meantime

BATTLING THE BOMBERS

Papa Hittgen had done everything in his power to lighten my task of finding the airfield. I finally landed, happy but sweating profusely, in the early morning hours at Venlo. I was received with shouts of joy by my friends who informed me that my Viennese had landed safely and reported my crash and his own rescue.

When we next met he naïvely said to me: "Well, sir, when you went into that power dive, you swore so terribly that I thought 'we've had it', and I took a quick powder."

"Without even saying goodbye," I replied.

"Hmm, Herr Leutnant, I was in a hurry, you know—but I'm glad to see you're still alive."

Chapter VI

THE LANDSIDE BEGINS

So far the British night raids had caused comparatively little damage. The German armament industry was still working at full blast and supplies were reaching the front line without interruption. The daily special communiqués on the successes of the Wehrmacht allowed us to hope for an early final victory. Deep in enemy territory, the German soldier was fighting with incomparable idealism and rolling the enemy ever further back to the gates of Moscow and Cairo; but the lines of communication grew longer and the occupied territories could only be lightly held. The home front worked like beavers to supply the soldiers at the front and to show them that they were not fighting on their own. The front line soldier believed that his dear ones were safe at home and this gave him courage. However, of what use is

BATTLING THE BOMBERS

courage in the long run against superior forces? As a result of Hitler's declaration of war on America in December, 1941, the British now had a new and powerful ally.

The British Isles experienced an American invasion such as had never before been seen: aircraft, tanks, ships, guns, trucks, ammunition, medical supplies and transports full of soldiers arrived in the English west coast harbours despite the great U-boat activity in the Atlantic. Airfields with mile-long runways sprang up like mushrooms. America's war production went into top gear and her endless reserves were poured into the battle. The American tempo determined the strategic raids on Germany. Where runways were lacking the Americans simply laid heavy closely-woven steel matting across meadows and fields. The same day American fighters ——Thunderbolts, Mustangs and Lightnings—took off from these temporary airfields—giving air cover to heavy bombers raiding the centre of Germany. The British flew by night and the Americans by day—a non-stop service. Impossible flying weather alone halted for a brief instant the offensive against the German home front.

The German fighter arm could not compete with this mass attack. In feverish haste new squadrons were formed, but of what use were young inexperienced pilots in night fighting? Many of them fell out of the sky without ever having seen an enemy. And yet the few squadrons fought bravely. The outward and return flights of the enemy were marked by the wrecks of burning aircraft. The British suffered serious losses but the gaps in their ranks were soon filled. Canadians, Australians, New Zealanders, South Africans and Americans reinforced the bomber groups

Each night death spread its wings over another German city; each morning brought tears of despair and terror of the approaching night. The night-fighter crews could no

BATTLING THE BOMBERS

longer think of sleep, for the enemy often came twice in one night. After the first mission we landed on some airfield, refuelled and took off once more against the enemy. Ops lasted from four to six hours. In the early morning the exhausted crews fell into their bunks and slept—until the Americans arrived in their silver birds. Alert—the night fighters also had to take part in the daylight defence. Hardly had they slept a few hours to rest their nerves after the excitement of the night than the air raid sirens roused them and they scrambled for their aircraft. The unequal struggle began—the American fast fighters against the slow clumsy German night fighters. The air throbbed with the drone of engines from bombers flying in close formation. Scores of fast fighters watched over their heavy charges, which flew on their course without deviation. As soon as the first German fighters appeared they dived on the enemy and within a few seconds a dogfight was in progress. In this mad chaos the night-fighter squadrons, in close formation, tried to approach the bombers. The gunners had the difficult task of keeping off the constant attacks of American fighters. It was a disastrous mêlée. Friend and foe hurtled in flames out of the sky, until in the late afternoon the American bomber stream turned on its course for home. Losses on both sides were appalling. Many of our night-fighter pilots who so far had fought magnificently in the darkness now fell in daylight combats. Until dusk we had a few hours rest and relaxation and then the performance began again.

Our No. 1 Night Fighter Wing in Venlo fought magnificently. Hauptmann Streib, Oberleutnants Thimmig, Frank, Knacke, Wandam, Griese and Loos were the wing aces. Night and day in bitter air battles Knacke engaged one Britisher after the other and won the Knight's Cross. Despite the British air supremacy the crews and the ground staff

BATTLING THE BOMBERS

continued to carry out their duties with enthusiasm. The comradeship between officers and crews and between the flying and the ground staff was magnificent. Each man who had been home on leave and experienced the night bombing carried out his duty more frantically and conscientiously than ever. And yet the gaping wounds no longer healed. Cities were pulverised and the bombing warfare gradually undermined the resistance of the people. Everything that men held dear went up in flames. Huge expanses of a city were often erased in a single night. Century-old buildings wtih priceless collections, castles, churches, schools, factories, private houses and stations disintegrated. The monstrous juggernaut of fire sucked the terrified people into its wake and consumed them.

The cities of Münster, Karlsruhe and Essen suffered grievously in the summer of 1942 from concentrated bombing attacks. One of my comrades who was on leave in Karlsruhe gave his own account of the 3rd September raid on his return.

At 02.10 hours the sirens wailed. Very few of the townspeople stumbled out of their warm beds and sought the protection of the air raid shelters. What was the good? In comparison with the big industrial cities Karlsruhe was unimportant and the British would at the most be making a feint or a nuisance attack. But suddenly, even the most cool headed citizen felt anxious as a deafening roar of engines made the air above this old Residenz town quiver. "The Tommies are over the city," ran the alarm cry through the streets and houses. The first bombs exploded in the centre of the city causing a panic among the population. Everyone rushed in despair to the air raid shelters and the wardens had the greatest difficulty in keeping order. Our flak gunners fired like maniacs into the night sky without inflicting any serious damage on the bombers. Street after street went up in flames. Tears stood in the eyes of the citizens on the following morning when they saw the tragic damage. The first doubts as to our war leadership began to rise and many people lost their faith in the Hitler regime. Wild rumours ran round the city. "I think," my friend who had returned from leave said at the end of his shattering report, "that the enemy has achieved his first objective: to destroy the morale of the home front."

How was this overwhelming attack by the Allied air forces to be halted? The problem remained unchanged: the discovery of the enemy by night. Out of the thousand oncoming bombers, flying in close formation through the sectors covered by individual night-fighter squadrons, only a fraction were caught in the searchlight beams and of these only a few were shot down by fighters. The majority of the bombers flew undetected on the outward and return journey from England over Holland and Belgium to Germany. The Night-Fighter Arm was too closely bound to the individual sectors and too limited in its radius of action. The British, by means of their secret service, had soon discovered the danger sectors and knew the weak spots in our defence from the reports of their own crews. What was the result? The Allied squadrons started from every airfield in England, assembled over a certain beacon in the North Sea and then flew at short intervals, almost goose-stepping towards the weakest night-fighter areas; then they crashed by sheer weight through this area like a broad stream driven through a narrow channel. Our whole night defence was crippled by these approach tactics. Since the broad zone of defence stretching from Paris over Flensburg was useless it had to become more elastic—but how? As long as the night-fighter

BATTLING THE BOMBERS

pilot had to rely on a machine being caught in the searchlights and could not find his opponent by his own efforts he was virtually helpless. The morale of the crews, which cruised around at night, unable to interfere while the Britishers broke through en masse perhaps twenty miles away, sank to zero.

And then at last came salvation. Berlin sent us the first night-fighter machines equipped with their own radar and moreover with an unlimited radius of action. Feverishly the electro-engineers had developed an apparatus which sent out electric beams on ultra-short waves into space. The path of the beam from transmitter to a metal object and back to the receiver took a fraction of a second, was measured by the apparatus and evaluated visibly on cathode ray tubes. This miracle machine aroused great excitement throughout the whole night-fighter arm. Rumours were rife and many people believed that machines would eventually be put into service equipped with "death rays." This rumour was not so wild as it appears, for although the Lichtenstein apparatus—it was known as "Li" in night-fighter circles—did not send out death rays, it seized the opponent with invisible arms and drew him towards itself as an octopus catches its prey. The deathblow from the night-fighter's cannon followed.

The radio operators were sent on courses to learn how to use the new instrument. Although the assembly and the instrument itself were highly complicated it was very simple to use. The outstanding feature of the Li was the long antennae in the nose of the plane, which the pilots soon nicknamed the "barbed wire". The field covered by these antennae was 30° above and below and 60° to port and starboard. The enemy aircraft was picked up by the apparatus at a distance corresponding to its own altitude.

BATTLING THE BOMBERS

Thus if the night fighter was flying at 13,000 feet the wireless operator could see the enemy plane on his screen at a distance of 4,400 yards.

Naturally the machine itself was not visible: only the so-called zigzags. Since the distance alone would be of little use to the night fighter, vertical and lateral zigzags appeared on two further screens making three pictures in all. For the wireless operator the handling of this apparatus, in addition to his other tasks such as radio compass and fix bearings, communication with the ground staff and over the R.T., entailed an enormous amount of extra work. Moreover, the light blue flickering cathode ray tubes dazzled the eyes so much, that the radio operator, after using the radar for half an hour, could no longer recognize the stars in a clear sky. Thus the pilot and the gunner had to keep an even greater watch on their sector. The installation of this apparatus also demanded increased co-operation and mutual understanding between the fighter controller and the wireless operator. Previously the pilot had been completely free to make his own decisions but now he had to rely on the reports of his operator and follow the course according to the radar measurements. At the same time the use of the Li resulted in a complete change in night fighter tactics. The sectors were retained but the direction of the fighters was now entrusted to high ranking ground officers. The tactics were basically altered so that the night fighter was no longer led into a certain limited sector but the entire ops group was assembled on the Channel coast above a heavy transmitting beacon which lay on the known approach route of the enemy. The wing commander agreed with their squadron commanders upon a secret frequency. The latter in turn got into communication with their crews: thus the C.O. could report to ground head

BATTLING THE BOMBERS

quarters in a comparatively short time that his wing was ready to take off.

In the most favourable conditions the entire night-fighter arm, graded at varying altitudes, circled above the beacon on the coast and was despatched from there at short intervals against the oncoming bomber stream. One might say that the cards had been well shuffled, and the Lichtenstein apparatus could begin to function. In addition to the earth picture or "earth zigzag" which appeared constant on all three tubes and signified that the enemy machine was only the distance of their own altitude away, the radio operator, once directed into the bomber stream, could now pick up the enemy machines. Pictorially described, the electric beams of the radar explored the ether and reported to the operator in fractions of a second the altitude, distance and quarter of the enemy aircraft. If, for example, 800 bombers and 100 night fighters were in the "stream" there was always the danger that instead of the opponent the radar beam would pick up one of their own fighters flying ahead. But the inventor had foreseen this and added an additional gadget which made it possible to distinguish between friend and foe.

With this new weapon the night fighter could pursue his opponent from the channel to the target and back to the English coast, as long as he remained in the bomber stream and did not run out of fuel. The ground stations continually gave the position of the raiders, so that the night fighters always knew the air situation and if necessary could be directed into the bomber stream once more. Various airfields were notified and turned on their lights as soon as a fighter got into trouble or ran out of juice. With the introduction of the Li an intensive battle was waged against the enemy in which every available night fighter took part.

BATTLING THE BOMBERS

The "migratory period" had set in for the crews and it was not unusual for pilots from France, Belgium, Germany or Denmark to meet on a Dutch airfield. In the grey light of dawn they then proceeded back to their own airfields. One night fighter was so absorbed in his task that he followed the enemy bomber stream to England and having run out of fuel, had to force land on a British airfield. For the Allies the introduction of this new apparatus was almost a catastrophe. The goosestep had suddenly became a death march.

On the 17th November, 1942, at about 23.00 hours there was great excitement among the crews at Venlo. The topic of the day was the Lichtenstein apparatus and the secret Operation "Adler."

The Division had given the order: "Various squadrons of night fighters equipped with the new radar will take off in close formation against the enemy. Shortly before the start the crews will be given the position of the enemy bomber stream and assemble over a beacon on the coast flashing the code signal LI. From this point onwards they will be introduced into the British bomber stream, which must be decimated before it reaches the target. Each crew is to pursue the enemy to the last drop of fuel."

The orders were quite clear. Oberleutnant Knacke and his wireless operator Heu ran over once more all the details and the possibilities which might arise on this new mission. All the airfields were carefully marked on the map, for as yet no one knew which city the British would attack that night. It might be Kiel or again it might be Frankfurt-am-Main. There was a feverish discussion as to the possibilities of success. "Not a single machine will get back to England," one of them maintained. This was obviously an exaggeration but everyone felt that there was something in the air. After their insignificant successes on recent ops and the terrible destruction of the German cities it was the obvious duty of the crews to make the most of this new invention.

23.20 hours. The coastal ground stations reported the start of strong bomber formations from the Midlands. Readiness for all thirty serviceable machines and crews. One operator reported that his Li was not working. A special radio car hastened over to the aircraft and checked the complicated mechanism. The fault was soon found and the machine was declared ready for ops.

23.45 hours. The loudspeaker reported: "The British bomber formations are assembling in Map Square 23. Long. 2° 20'; Lat. 52° 32'. Strength of the formation: circa 600 aircraft. Altitude 15,000 feet. All aircraft proceed to beacon Li at Scheveningen on the Channel Coast."

23.46 hours. Oberleutnant Knacke was the first to take off. He turned on to course 200 without making a circuit round the field. He switched off his navigating lights and his machine was swallowed up in the darkness.

A clear starry sky lay over Holland. Ideal weather for night fighters. Knacke did not spare his aircraft and rose at 18 feet per second to the prescribed altitude.

Unteroffizier Heu called his squadron mates on the intercom. "Buzzard 5 from Buzzard 1. Come in."

"Buzzard 1 from Buzzard 5. Victor, message received. Am on course 200."

One after the other the planes reported. Knacke called up the C.O. and received a reply. Hauptmann Streib ordered complete radio silence to prevent the British having any suspicions of their presence. The ground station reported three other night-fighter wings in the air.

24.10 hours. Orders to attack. "All aircraft fly on course 180. The leading bombers are flying over the coast west of

BATTLING THE BOMBERS

Rotterdam on course 90. Probable objective the Ruhr. Enemy altitude 16,500 feet."

Oberleutnant Knacke turned on his radar, set his course at 180 and came down to 16,500 feet. Within five minutes he would meet the leading bombers. The first real test of the new radar eye had begun. Unteroffizier Heu eagerly watched the pictures on the cathode ray tubes. At the outset only the ground zig-zag appeared giving a regular jagged line on the lower screen of the tube. Tension rose, for six minutes flying time had already elapsed.

Then the miracle occurred. From starboard to port a fine jagged line travelled above the ground picture into the side cathode ray tube: the enemy. Heu was wild with excitement. He immediately gave his pilot a change of course to 90°, and behold, as the machine turned the enemy line retreated from starboard to port and remained in the centre of the tube. The bomber was therefore directly ahead. The distance tube showed 4,000 yards and the altitude tube 16,350 feet. Knacke could not believe that the Britisher was already pinpointed at this great distance. He peered out in the direction of his opponent but could not see him, for the vision of the human in the dark is not more than 100 to 200 yards. His nerves were at breaking point. Would the Tommy be able to break out of his radar field? No, for the crews were still flying calmly towards the defence zone and would only be at action stations once the first searchlight was turned on. The pilot was taking no avoiding action. Knacke gave full throttle: the distance deceased from 4,000 to 3,500 to 3,000 and to 2,500 yards.

Suddenly Heu reported a new contact at 2,000 yards distance. A British machine had crossed their field slowly, from north to south. For a moment Knacke was uncertain which opponent to pursue; then he decided upon the nearest bomber. The big enemy zig-zags showed up wonderfully in the tubes. The machine had begun to weave and was now travelling on the screen alternately from port to starboard and back. Could the crew have noticed anything? That was impossible. The distance decreased to 500 and to 300 yards.

Cautiously Knacke throttled down and looked out on all sides. Heu gave him the final Li readings: "Opponent 200 yards ahead, 50 feet above us." Then he could no longer endure the light in the apparatus. But the Britisher was still invisible to the human eye.

Three pairs of eyes scanned the sky for his shadow. The situation was not without its dangers: there were always the dangers of a collision or of being spotted first. Knacke grew nervous since he still could not see the enemy. Heu looked once more in his apparatus. The zig-zags were now gigantic on the distance screen. The bomber must now be very close to the pursuing night fighter. Knacke gave a start. Straight ahead and a little above him he had caught sight of the barely visible shadow of a four-engined bomber. Now he must take care. The Britisher had not spotted him.

The mighty shark's fins on the tail unit were clearly outlined against the night sky. A Short Stirling! She carried eight to ten tons of explosives in her bomb bays ready to drop on the Ruhr. Knacke did not hesitate for a second but waded in. Bright flames spurted from the engines and tanks. A second burst tore open the fuselage and probably killed the crew. In the ghostly light he could see the red, white and blue circles on the body of the aircraft just before it plunged with its bomb load into the depths. This kill had the effect of a nightmare beam upon his fellow pilots

BATTLING THE BOMBERS

now attacking the bomber stream. The plane exploded with a bright scarlet flash in the harbour of Rotterdam.

An now a terrifying half hour began for the enemy. Everywhere in the sky could be seen the flash of tracers from heavy machine guns and cannon. Three, four, five enemy bombers hurtled on fire earthwards. The path of their flight from Rotterdam to the Ruhr was strewn with blazing wrecks. The Li machine had proved itself to be a precision instrument. Within half an hour Knacke had shot down four bombers. Then he had a terrifying experience. Heu reported a contact at 2,000 yards. Knacke attacked at full speed. He caught up his opponent and in the darkness suddenly caught sight of the British rear gunner's Perspex cockpit. In his excitement Knacke fired immediately into the full petrol tanks. The British rear gunner lost his head, left his machine guns and baled out, landing right in the propeller of the pursuing night fighter. There was a dull thud, which made Knacke's plane shudder. The engine began to vibrate so badly that he had to cut it out. He landed his clumsy Me. 110 at Venlo on one engine. Mechanics rushed over and lit up the machine. By the light of their torches they could still see traces of blood and hair on the propeller. Strips of uniform were hanging on the antennae of the Li. The fate of the British gunner upset everyone. Over a hundred bombers lay that night as wrecks on Dutch soil. The invisible Li rays had broken up a mass attack on the Ruhr that night and had been disastrous to the English crews.

Obituary: Oberleutnant Reinhold Knacke, the ace of No. 1 Night-Fighter Wing, was born in Strelitz on 1st January, 1919. The young Squadron Leader shot down fortythree of the enemy by night in bitter air combats over Holland. His successes were several times reported in the Wehrmacht communiqués.

BATTLING THE BOMBERS

But the operations eventually began to fray his nerves. Knacke felt this and led an incredibly ascetic life. He neither drank nor smoked, and in the rest periods kept fit by playing games with his fellow pilots. One February night in 1943 the fate of this modest conscientious flying officer was sealed. His C.O. had just recommended him for the oak leaves to the Knight's Cross but the decoration was awarded to him posthumously. After a bitter fight with a four-engined Halifax, the enemy bomber and the night fighter plunged together into the depths. The British rear gunner opened fire at exactly the same moment as Knacke and the bursts on both sides were fatal. In the early morning the troops found the crews and debris of both machines lying next to each other in a field.

Chapter VII

THE CALM BEFORE THE STORM

DURING THIS successful period with the new radar apparatus against the R.A.F. I was posted in December, 1942, with No. 3 Squadron of No. 1 Night-Fighter Wing to Parchim. This order came as a complete surprise, for during my eighteen months with this wing I had grown very attached to it. The squadron successes and the tough times we had experienced together as well as the moments of triumph had forged strong bonds between the pilots.

Parchim is in Mecklenburg and so far had been left unscathed by the war. The landscape and the inhabitants radiated peace and contentment. After the exciting ops in Holland I felt as though I had been sent on permanent leave. The Parchim C.O. was obviously delighted to see us arrive. The full sheds were cleared of the old training machines and now served to house brand new night-fighter types which had just arrived from Gotha. The extremely well-equipped workshop was adapted to service our Messerschmitts. The entire airfield installations were renovated to deal with night-fighter activities. By Christmas, 1942, the wing was fully equipped and at full complement. The backbone of No. 3 Night-Fighter Wing 6 was the veteran operational squadron from Venlo. The officer commanding this new night-fighter wing was Hauptmann Schönert, an officer of experience. Nearly all the crews were fresh from training school. We flew every night and no time was lost, for even the younger pilots realized why they were in Parchim—to protect the German capital from the coming terror raids.

Most of the boys from the flying schools were magnificent airmen. Flying was in their blood. Hauptmann Schönert realized his luck in being able to prepare his crews for ops in peace and quiet, without enemy interference. What would have happened to these young pilots had they been flung immdiately into action as soon as they left school? The answer had already been seen in the West. Night after night the youngsters did not return while the veterans continued to pile up their victories: and yet the "rookies" in Parchim did not realize how lucky they were. On the contrary, they cursed this godforsaken hole and the boring peace-time conditions. Hauptmann Schönert used to say: "It is a fine thing to die a hero's death, but you are far more use to your country as a pilot."

In the West the battle between the armies coninued with undiminished vigour. In May, 1943, a message came from the Division: "The West needs reinforcements." Since in

BATTLING THE BOMBERS

the short summer nights only attacks on the Ruhr could be envisaged, Fighter Corps assembled the experienced crews on the Dutch and Belgian airfields. I, too, was posted to the West. My crew was delighted. The fellows who remained behind were very depressed when they said goodbye to us. Our crates were stuffed to bursting point with everything the airman needs when he is posted—wireless set, a dog, washing and toilet utensils, "Schnapps cupboard," and a good many other things. Space was cramped in the aircraft. The radio operator and gunner sat huddled together in the rear cockpit. Our Me. 110 looked more like a furniture van than a streamlined night fighter. Hedgehopping over the airfield we dipped our wings in farewell to those who remained behind and set our course westwards.

At dusk, about 19.33 hours, I landed on the big airfield of Gilze near Breda and reported to the C.O. Hauptmann Frank, an old friend from my Venlo days. It was a pleasant reunion. Among my new mates were the successful long-distance night fighters Leutnants Heinz Strünning, Bussmann and Oberfeldwebel Gildner. Strünning, with Cologne wit, told me of his experiences as a night fighter over England. In 1941 and 1942 these courageous pilots hovered over the English airfields and shot down the bombers just as they came in to land. "Uncle Heini," as we called him because he was older than ourselves, relived his adventures as he told them to us.

"Boys," he said jestingly, "there were so many Tommies circling the airfield that we could have knocked them out of the skies with our caps."

One evening in July, 1943, we were all in our bomb-proof dug-out waiting for ops. Strünning entered and burst out: "Boys, have I had a laugh! A real blue-blooded aristocrat blew in today. But let me sit down."

Suddenly we heard the faint drone of engines which increased in strength until they were directly overhead. A loud hiss and we all lay flat on the floor. Bombs. The light flickered and went out. Crump! The next stick was quite close. By rights we should have jumped into the trench, but no one gave it a thought. In the dug-out we were protected from splinters—and why should the bombs fall directly on the roof?

Uncle Heini lit a candle and went on with his story. "I was sitting with Hauptmann Frank this afternoon when a tall, thin captain strolled in. 'Good morning,, Frank,' he said with a drawl. 'I'm Wittgenstein, and I've been posted to your squadron. What's cooking? Where is there something to shoot down?' He's in a hurry, I thought to myself. At the same moment he introduced himself to me. 'Ah, my friend,' said our O.C., rather bewildered, 'I suppose you're Prince Wittgenstein, the former bomber pilot?' 'Quite right, my dear Frank. But drop the Prince, just call me Wittgenstein. Have my machine put near control so that I can take off at once.'

"A madman, I thought, as I took my leave. Once outside I got into conversation with the Prince's crew. Among other things they told me that their princely coachman had recently made his radio operator stand to attention in the plane and confined him to his quarters for three days because he had lost the picture in his screen during a mission. Since he shot down three bombers shortly afterwards he pardoned the man and awarded him the Iron Cross First Class. All this took place at 15,000 feet, right in the middle of the English bomber stream. 'There's no holding the Prince

BATTLING THE BOMBERS

once he's in the air,' they said. 'He takes off like a maniac and only lands when he hasn't a drop of juice left.'"

The following day I had the pleasure of flying with him in Beaver Sector. When we met over the beacon he sent me the following message: "You stick here by the beacon, I'm off hunting."

Since he was a captain and I was only a lieutenant I could not disobey, but I went off hunting all the same.

Obituary. Heinrich Prince zu Sayn-Wittgenstein was one of the most successful night-fighter pilots and his name was bracketed with those of Major Streib and Lent. But the ambition of this eager and outstanding airman was to be head of the night-fighter élite. Spurred on by his need for action, the young Group Commander shot down eighty-four enemy bombers in tough air battles. But his eighty-fourth victory—actually his fifth kill on the night of the 21st January, 1944—led him not to his coveted position but to his death. Directly after his fifth victory that night he was attacked and shot down by a British night fighter. The Prince gave orders to his crew to bale out and tried to save his aircraft. He failed. Recognizing the danger too late, he baled out just before the burning machine crashed. On the following day his body was found near the wreckage.

Major Heinrich Prince zu Sayn-Wittgenstein, born on the 14th August, 1916, in Copenhagen, decorated with the Oak Leaves and Swords to the Knight's Cross, will be remembered by all night-fighter pilots as a courageous and exemplary airman.

A warm mild breeze blew through the musty barracks and attracted us outside. Engines were being revved up at the far end of the airfield.

BATTLING THE BOMBERS

"Ha-ha," said Uncle Heini, "those are our remaining bombers which have not yet been destroyed on the ground. The poor crews are now off to England. I recently had a chat with one of their N.C.O. pilots. They're really to be pitied. In the old days they set out in armadas of between 400 and 600 aircraft and today there are only about 100 of them left. Moreover, those old crates are out of date and an easy prey for the British night fighters. If thirty of them set out tonight, probably only twenty would return."

Our proud bomber formations in the West had sunk lamentably. Some of them were sent to the Eastern Front and the rest were decimated night after night without receiving sufficient reinforcements. The Allies had won air supremacy not only over the British Isles but also over German territory.

Even the simple soldier now began to reflect upon the failure of the Luftwaffe. His incipient doubts, however, were still stifled by skilful propaganda. The high-ranking Nazi officers gave lectures on the new V-1 and V-2 weapons. "There is no further need now," they insisted, "for us to fly to England. We shall soon bring the British to their knees with our V-1. Until then the German soldier must stick it out and do his best to protect the Fatherland from further losses. Long live the Führer." Always the same words: "Stick it out, stick it out!"

The night-fighter squadrons really gave of their best. From the group captains to the youngest corporal pilots they took off night after night against the enemy. The ground staff taxed themselves to the limit to get all the machines serviceable before nightfall. But in the Machine Age all effort and sacrifices on the part of the squadrons are of no avail when they lag behind the enemy in technical progress. What we needed were faster and better day

BATTLING THE BOMBERS

fighters, bombers or night fighters. Was it not a disgrace to our leaders that the Tommy could fly longer and at a greater speed over the Reich than our own fighters? In 1940 our Me. 109s and Focke-Wulfs fought on even terms with the Hurricanes and Spitfires. But how was it now in 1943? They still took off in the same Me. 109s and Focke-Wulfs—although in improved types—against faster enemy machines such as Thunderbolts, Mustangs, Mosquitoes and Lightnings. The Allies now used their Hurricanes and Spits as training machines. We asked ourselves daily why the Luftwaffe was not equipped with turbo-jets, the plans of which already lay in Professor Messerschmitt's locker in 1941. Were they going to delay until it was perhaps too late? These were our gloomy thoughts as we sat waiting for the next night ops.

The British had hardly started than we received the order: "Readiness for all machines." The Tommy was airborne.

00.50 hours. Orders to take-off. I flew on a direct course to Schauwen Island and climbed to 15,000 feet. Beaver Headquarters reported the first radar contacts. 01.00 hours. My radio operator, Facius, reported a Tommy 1,000 yards away flying due west. Full throttle! The enemy machine swiftly approached. We were now directly over the coast. The sea glittered pale in the moonlight and the land lay in complete darkness. My Me. 110 was caught in the first propeller slipstreams. Now I had to keep my eyes skinned.

Facius gave the latest reports: "Enemy fifty yards ahead at our altitude."

Within a matter of seconds I saw the glowing exhaust pipes—eight of them. Ah! a four-engined bomber. I did a shallow dive until I was 150 feet below the Tommy. Facius

BATTLING THE BOMBERS

had already recognized the type—a Halifax. I attacked and hit the left wing with my first burst. The flames spurted from the tanks and I could clearly see the red, white and blue circles. The burning bomber hurtled like a comet down to earth and the hunt went on. 01.43 hours. Another picture on our screen. Facius did a good job. Slowly we stalked the opponent. 1,000 yards . . . 600 . . . 200 . . . 100 . . . and I could already see the dark shadow. Another Halifax. A minute later this bomber, too, had been despatched on fire. Silence then reigned over the air.

A few moments later Beaver Headquarters reported a heavy attack on Cologne. The dispersed British squadrons met over Cologne. I received orders from the ground station to circle over the Beaver beacon and to wait for their return flight.

In the far distance on the west horizon we could see a bright glow in the sky: the bombs were falling on the cathedral city. Beaver soon reported the first returning bombers. Long before they reached the coast the British lost height in order to cross the Channel at a greater speed and reach the haven of their own coast.

"Falcon 10 from Beaver. Come in."

I gave my altitude and course.

"Falcon 10. Fly on course 280. Enemy aircraft at 9,000 feet. Couriers losing height."

I reacted at once and set off in pursuit. The distance was still 6,000 yards. I dived steeply and gave more throttle. Facius set the aerial arms of the Li in action, exploring the air around him. Suddenly jagged lines appeared on the screen.

Beaver reported: "Enemy flying at full speed for the coast. Give her full throttle."

BATTLING THE BOMBERS

"Do you think he'll get away?" asked my radio operator.

"No, he mustn't get away," I replied.

The engines roared and my speed rose to 310 m.p.h. Slowly we caught up with the enemy. "He's turned," reported Facius. The jagged lines on the cathode-ray tubes kept swinging from port to starboard and back. We were already over the sea at 6,000 feet. I gambled everything on one card and set the throttle at full power. At this stress the engines would only last for a bare five minutes. Facius stopped his watch. My plane bucked and shuddered. The vibrations and the rough running of the engines were communicated to the crew. Those were the moments of greatest tension. At any moment one could reckon with a disaster.

Facius reported calmly: "We're closing in fast. Enemy 1,000 yards ahead."

Now one of us had only ten minutes more to live, for there was no chance of rescue over the sea. One of us must go down, for that was the law of warfare.

"Six hundred yards now," reported Facius. "Enemy flying on the same course and losing height."

A swift glance at my altimeter: it showed 3,600 feet. We were at a ticklish height. It was only a matter of seconds when one had to bale out of a burning machine. The parachute needed time to open, the Mae West had to be blown up before bailing out or else it sank like a lump of lead.

"Distance 400 yards."

Well, no use thinking about it. Bright moonlight astern favoured the Tommy. He had the greatest chance of spotting us first. For this reason I took up my position on his quarter, so as not to receive a full burst from the rear gunner's armaments.

BATTLING THE BOMBERS

Facius reported: "Distance 150 yards, altitude 2,400, enemy dead ahead."

And there he was! The bomber's shark fins gleamed in the bright moonlight. At the same moment the Tommy had spotted me and banked savagely to port. The life-and-death struggle began. Hardly was I in firing position than the bomber zoomed. His wing surfaces grew enormous, as though appealing for help to the dark night sky. But I kept on his tail. As he zoomed the enemy's fuselage came fully into my sights. I fired but in a flash he recognized the danger and went into a steep dive. The sweat was pouring down my cheeks. My altimeter showed only 900 feet. The British pilot pulled out just above the water at the very last moment. Now he was too low to dive again. The pilot weaved like a maniac to disturb my aim. The crew were firing madly with all their guns and the tracers framed my machine. Now it was a question of keeping a cool head. I dived right down to the water. As a result of this manoeuvre the Tommy probably lost sight of me. For a moment he flew on even keel, then I zoomed and pressed the button of my cannon and machine-guns. A giant flame spurted from the port petrol tank and the bomber crashed with its crew into the sea.

My crew breathed with relief. They had lived through these anxious moments without being able to do anything. No one said a word as we circled above the scene of the crash. A bright-red gurgle in the water and once more darkness and silence. Slowly I climbed to 3,000 feet and flew in the direction of the Dutch coast. Facius called Beaver Headquarters, but they did not hear us for our fight had carried us too far out to sea. After this third victory I was all in. Only one idea remained in my head: to get home, to land and to sleep. At last Beaver replied.

BATTLING THE BOMBERS

"Beaver from Falcon 10," I called. "Third kill. A Vickers Wellington shot down over the sea in Map Square IG 33. On my way home."

At 02.47 hours I touched down on the flarepath at Gilzerijn. I hardly heard the congratulations of my fellow pilots.

In the huts I met Heinz Strünning. "My God, Johnen," he said, "I was over Cologne. It was a gruesome sight. The whole city was a sea of flames. Let's hope my wife and children are still alive. If things go on like this we shall soon be in a real mess." This was the first time that I had seen our cheerful Heini look serious. We wandered slowly back to our huts. The night wind cooled our heated foreheads.

"Good night, Heini. Off again tomorrow, I suppose."

"Night," he replied. "But I hope it won't be over Cologne."

By a lucky coincidence I landed once more at my old station, Venlo. What a change I found in No. 1 Night-Fighter Wing. My former C.O., Major Streib, was delighted to see me. Very few of his trusty veterans were still alive. The men with experience had been dispersed in all directions and formed the backbone of the night-fighter wings from Paris to Flensburg. New faces greeted me. The once chivalrous combat waged by the night fighters, which spoke well for the fair, disciplined training of the airmen, under the pressure of the terrible losses inflicted on the civilian population by round-the-clock bombing had developed into a ruthless warfare in which no quarter was given. The pilots' faces had grown hard and no trace of youthfulness remained.

Major Streib, the most successful night-fighter wing commander, had now shot down sixty-six enemy bombers and had been awarded the Oak Leaves with Swords to his

BATTLING THE BOMBERS

Knight's Cross. The previous night, within a short time, he had managed to increase his score by five thanks to our new night-fighter plane, the He. 219. Later he met with an accident on landing.

This Heinkel type, originally developed, thanks to the energy of General Kammhuber, in co-operation between Night-Fighter Command, troops and industry, still had teething troubles. Although the pilots' demands for high speed, powerful armament, good range and visibility had been fulfilled, this prototype developed faults in design. At high speeds the tail unit began to wobble. The fuselage had been lengthened to overcome this.

Streib flew this machine from its seventh test flight onwards. On the previous night the He. 219 had been in action for the first time. Five bombers were brought down. But on landing, although the machine had not been hit, various instruments were put out of action. The wing flaps also failed to function. They could be lowered to Landing Position but immediately rose to Normal Flight. Streib, therefore, was obliged to land at a very great speed. When the machine touched down with a bump on the concrete runway the starboard engine broke away from the wing. There was a deafening report. The He. literally broke in pieces; wings and fuselage collapsed, the Perspex cockpit came away from the body and whirled with the pilot fifty yards through the air. Fortunately Streib was uninjured. The fire-engine and ambulance men hurried up to free his radio operator, Unteroffizier Fischer, from the wreckage. By some miracle, he, too, was unhurt. The pair of them were astonishingly lucky!

Chapter VIII

THE TINFOIL ENEMY

On the 27th July, 1943, there was something in the air. The early warnings from the Freya apparatus on the Channel coast indicated a large-scale British raid. In the late afternoon various flak units, night-fighter wings and civilian air-raid posts had been given orders to have their full complement at action stations. What were the British up to? What city that night would be the victim of these well-prepared raids? Every ominous presentiment was to be fulfilled that night. In all ignorance, the night-fighter squadrons took off against the British bombers, whose leaders were reported over Northern Holland.

I was on ops and flew in the direction of Amsterdam. On board everything was in good order and the crew was in a cheerful mood. Radio operator Facius made a final check and reported that he was all set. The ground stations kept calling the night fighters, giving them the positions of the bombers. That night, however, I felt that the reports were being given hastily and nervously. It was obvious no one knew exactly where the enemy was or what his objective would be. An early recognition of the direction was essential so that the night fighters could be introduced as early as possible into the bomber stream. But the radio reports kept contradicting themselves. Now the enemy was over Amsterdam and then suddenly west of Brussels, and a moment later they were reported far out to sea in Map Square 25. What was to be done? The uncertainty of the ground stations was communicated to the crews. Since this game of hide-and-seek went on for some time I thought: To hell with them all, and flew straight to Amsterdam. By the time I arrived over the capital the air position was still in a complete muddle. No one knew where the British were, but all the pilots were reporting pictures on their screens. I was no exception. At 15,000 feet my sparker announced the first enemy machine in his Li. I was delighted. I swung round on to the bearing in the direction of the Ruhr, for in this way I was bound to approach the stream. Facius proceeded to report three or four pictures on his screens. I hoped that I should have enough ammunition to deal with them!

Then Facius suddenly shouted: "Tommy flying towards us at a great speed. Distance decreasing . . . 2,000 yards, 1,500 . . . 1,000 . . . 500 . . ."

I was speechless. Facius already had a new target. "Perhaps it was a German night fighter on a westerly course," I said to myself and made for the next bomber.

It was not long before Facius shouted again: "Bomber coming for us at a hell of a speed. 2,000 . . . 1,000 . . . 500 . . . He's gone."

"You're crackers, Facius," I said jestingly.

But I soon lost my sense of humour for this crazy performance was repeated a score of times and finally I gave Facius such a rocket that he was deeply offended.

This tense atmosphere on board was suddenly interrupted by a ground station calling: "Hamburg, Hamburg. A thousand enemy bombers over Hamburg. Calling all night fighters, calling all night fighters. Full speed for Hamburg."

I was speechless with rage. For half an hour I had been weaving about in a presumed bomber stream and the bombs were already falling on Germany's great port. It was a long way to Hamburg. The Zuider Zee, the Ems and the Weser disappeared below us and Hamburg appeared in the distance. The city was blazing like a furnace. It was a horrifying sight. On my arrival over the city the ground station was already reporting the homeward flight of the enemy in the direction of Heligoland. Too late! The flak gunners had already ceased to fire and the gruesome work of destruction had been accomplished. In low spirits we flew back to our airfield.

How could the German defences have been rendered so impotent? We know today. The British had procured an example of our successful Li apparatus and had found the counter-measure. With ridiculous strips of tinfoil they could now lure the entire German night-fighter arm on to false trails and reach their own target unmolested. It was a simple yet brilliant idea. As is well known, radar works on a determined ultra-short wave frequency. By dropping these strips of tinfoil the British jammed this frequency. In this way the air goal was achieved and for the night fighter the bomber had once more become as invisible as it had been before the invention of the Lichtenstein apparatus.

While the main bomber stream far out to sea was flying towards Hamburg, smaller formations had flown over Holland and Belgium to Western Germany, dropping millions of tinfoil strips. These "Laminetta" appeared on the German screens as enemy bombers and put various ground stations out of action. The smaller formations, according to schedule, next dropped enormous quantities of flares—the famous Christmas trees—over various cities in the Ruhr. A few bombs were also dropped. The night fighters streaked towards these signs of attack from all directions, looking in vain for the bomber stream.

In the meantime the leaders of the British main raiding

BATTLING THE BOMBERS

force reached Heligoland unhindered and dropped more strips, putting the ground detectors out of action. At one blow both ground and air defence had been paralysed. In daylight on the following morning, whole areas of Holland, Belgium and Northern Germany were strewn with these strips of foil. Certain people maintained that they were poisonous and that they would kill all the cattle. The innocuousness of these small pieces of tinfoil on the ground was soon apparent, but in the air they were deadly—fatal for the life of a whole city.

A few days later we heard further details of the agony of this badly hit city. The raging fires in a high wind caused terrific damage and the grievous loss of human life outstripped any previous raids. All attempts to extinguish them proved fruitless and technically impossible. The fires spread unhindered, causing fiery storms which reached heats of 1,000°, and speeds approaching gale force. The narrow streets of Hamburg with their countless backyards were favourable to the flames and there was no escape. As the result of a dense carpet bombing, large areas of the city had been transformed into a single sea of flame within half an hour. Thousands of small fires joined up to become a giant conflagration. The fiery wind tore the roofs from the houses, uprooted large trees and flung them into the air like blazing torches. The inhabitants took refuge in the air-raid shelters, in which later they were burned to death or suffocated. In the early morning, thousands of blackened corpses could be seen in the burned-out streets. In Hamburg now one thought was uppermost in every mind—to leave the city and to abandon the battlefield. During the following nights, until the 3rd August, 1943, the British returned and dropped on the almost defenceless city about 3,000 blockbusters, 1,200 land-mines, 25,000 H.E., 3,000,-

BATTLING THE BOMBERS

000 incendiaries, 80,000 phosphorus bombs and 500 phosphorus drums; 40,000 men were killed, a further 40,000 wounded and 900,000 were homeless or missing. This devastating raid on Hamburg had the effect of a red light on all the big German cities and on the whole German people. Everyone felt it was now high time to capitulate before any further damage was done. But the High Command insisted that the "total war" should proceed. Hamburg was merely the first link of a long chain of pitiless air attacks made by the Allies on the German civilian population.

Shortly after our return from the West to Parchim, we had a little celebration, where the drink flowed freely. A fellow pilot from Essen, Peter Spoden, who was very popular in the mess, had to keep going down to the cellar. The "old man", Hauptmann Schönert, was on free and easy terms with the whole mess. He remembered his own youth and spoke enthusiastically of his life as a sailor. During a lull in the party he suddenly stood up, grabbed one of us by the shoulders and dragged him to the window. The last rays of the evening sun were breaking over the cloud banks on the horizon and staining the heavens scarlet. The sky was a riot of colour, from the most delicate blue to fiery red on the rising cloud bank. The evening had fallen and deep peace lay over the land. The C.O. opened the window to let in the cool air. The pine woods were fragrant. He puffed his cigar with relish and turned to us with a smile.

"Boys, you've bitten off a pretty hard chunk. You get into your crates and are swallowed up in the darkness. Some of you return from single combats at thousands of feet above the tortured, burning earth. Each of you flings his life without a murmur into the scales. A bloody hard life.

"At the age of twenty I lived a carefree happy one. I

BATTLING THE BOMBERS

sailed the seven seas as a ship's boy and learned to appreciate and love other nations. You could find good pals everywhere. We were all flung together in our cargo boats—Britishers, Norwegians, Danes and Germans. At first the atmosphere was very cold, but once we had the first storm behind us, we smiled at each other. During the first days at sea it was each man for himself, and yet as soon as we began to feel homesick we grew closer to each other. Soon we were pals and brothers. To hell with all prejudices! Here in the howling storm, when the huge breakers washed the decks and Father Death stood in the bows, was to be found the real League of Nations. We laughed at the raging seas.

"And this laugh meant confidence and mutual aid in life and death. When the gale blew itself out we had a breathing space and we had been granted a new lease of life. On reaching our home port after many months, we had become a community which recognized no difference of people, race or speech. With heavy hearts we said farewell in the hope that we should never forget comrades who had shared our joys and griefs.

"I have found the same comradeship among you. We, too, are faced with the same dangers and yet . . . there's something eating me." There was a bitter look on his face as he said these words. "We are destroying ourselves. Our fight is not against the powers of nature for the good of humanity but an attempt to destroy life with all the new weapons of science.

"Do not men of our race—perhaps the fair-haired Britishers with whom I sailed in the Bay of Biscay and made friends—sit in their bombers, night after night, turning our cities to ruins? Each does his duty. But don't we thereby aggravate our hatred? At night we see only the enemy bomber and its bright red, white and blue circles. Our cities burn. The bomber must be brought down at all costs, and when it crashes we crow. We only see the bomber burning and not the crew. We only see the emblem laid low, not the youngsters hanging on their straps in their death agony.

"And then perhaps one day you meet a Tommy who has baled out. You meet him down below. His eyes have lost the harsh glint of battle. You shake hands and this handshake is the beginning of a comradeship, born of a life and death struggle. Gratefully he accepts the cigarette you offer. The barrier that divided us has fallen and two men stand facing each other. Hostility and propaganda have made them enemies but the common danger of battle has made them friends. Just as here, in a small way, hatred is changed to friendship, may the racial hatred also turn to friendship. But the iron carapace in which the nations shroud themselves, the outward symbols of which are emblems and threats, must be swept away, for the more the modern world uses science, the bloodier will the battles become. The more man takes refuge behind armour plating and steel, the greater will be his will to destruction. For this reason this bloody murder must come to an end. The peoples must lay aside their blood-stained armour unless the whole world is to be destroyed. All the peoples of the world could live in peace, and this path must be taken together and protected so that they could all rise in judgment against anyone who left the path. . . ." Hauptmann Schönert looked up at the darkening sky.

Short indeed were these hours of relaxation for the menace of the British hung like a sword of Damocles over the German cities. They were trying to destroy the heart of Germany from the air. All of us were living under the spell of the approaching catastrophe. This rest period

BATTLING THE BOMBERS

had to be used for training the newcomers. Night after night we flew, practised and trained, until the recruits could handle their machines with the precision of a sleepwalker.

Chapter IX

FIGHTER CONTROL

THE DEADLY tinfoil strips came as a tremendous shock to the whole Signals Service. But the German inventive spirit reacted swiftly and in feverish haste our radio specialists brought out a new radar apparatus, the SN 2, a development of the Lichtenstein. Outwardly the SN 2 was easy to recognize on our machines because the antennae were larger. The nickname "barbed wire" was now even more appropriate. The SN 2 worked on several ultra-short waves so that the operator could change his waves when one particular frequency was jammed. But it required sensitive fingers and a great deal of practice to get the enemy bomber clearly on the screen of the new instrument. The crews flew night after night, to improve contact between the pilot and the wireless operator. The C.O. had ordered a practice operation for that particular night.

The large shed doors were set in motion by pressing on an electric button. The harsh light streamed out on to the tarmac in front of the shed and was gradually swallowed up by the huge airfield. The white-painted night fighters stood there with their threatening cannon muzzles blackened by the gunpowder. The aerials on the nose of the machine looked like thin, waving tentacles. The shed was filled with the smell of petrol and oil. A few mechanics were working

BATTLING THE BOMBERS

conscientiously by a spotlight on the engines of C 9 ES, on whose tail unit were painted seventeen bands, representing the number of victories.

"Stop work," ordered the Chief Mechanic. "The squadron is off on target-spotting practice. All the machines to the runway."

In the meantime other mechanics had appeared from their huts and were removing the tarpaulins from the planes. The cockpit windows were quickly cleaned, for the slightest speck of dust on the Perspex disturbed the night-fighter pilot. How often had a young pilot streaked at full speed after one of these specks of dust until he had to admit that the shadow he thought he saw against the bright night sky drew no nearer. In this way precious time was lost.

Heavy tractors drove up and towed the aircraft out of the sheds on hawsers. Parachute orderlies fetched the air lifebelts from the drying room and laid them carefully in the cockpit ready to be put on.

"*Achtung! Achtung!* Report on the air situation. A few single fast bombers have entered West German territory. No formations reported. Weather report: high pressure belt over Western Europe. Light cirrus between 15,000 and 18,000 feet. Wind from 180 to 200°, 6 to 14 m.p.h. One day after full moon. The following aircraft will take part in target-spotting practice: AS to Sector Heron; DS to Sector Swan; FS to Sector Doe; HS to Sector Bear. KS remains in reserve. Start 01.00 hours. End of message."

The lights went out in the shed. Bright moonlight lay over the airfield and made the aircraft look like ghosts. The leading mechanics jumped on to the machines with their torches and made a final check-up of all the instruments and switches.

"All set?" asked the Chief. "Warm the engines up, then.

BATTLING THE BOMBERS

Watch your cooling indicator. Today in this warm air put your radiator flaps full out."

The control lamp went on in the tail. The Chief pressed on the self-starter of the starboard engine. "Contact."

"Contact," replied the mechanics and got out of the way of the propeller.

The hum of the power starter grew louder. The blades jerked and bright flames from the unused petrol spurted from the exhaust dimmers. The mixture was too rich. Full throttle and the engine fired. After a brief rattle it settled down to smooth running. Everything in order. The performance was repeated with the port engine and now they were both running smoothly. Six hundred horse-power was housed in each of these steel masterpieces of precision. At intervals a shudder ran through the whole machine as the petrol and oil pressure gradually rose. A rapid throttling back of the engines and then the mechanic gradually pushed the throttle full home. The engines roared and it was impossible to hear a word. The rev. counter needle sprang from 1,500 to 2,700 to 2,800 r.p.m. No faulty plugs or suspicious noises to be heard. The Chief contentedly reduced the gas. A red flash of his torch informed the second mechanic, who jumped beneath the gondola and pulled out the cut-out device. The blades turned counter-clockwise. Soon all the aircraft had been checked. The Chief could report to H.Q. that everything was set.

Here, in the central combat station, the brain of the night-fighter arm, were hundreds of telephone lines. Hardly a minute passed before a pilot somewhere in the dark sky was given the course and position of an aircraft. In a matter of seconds the fighter was thrown on to a big frosted glass panel as a bright green dot, with his exact position, course and altitude. As soon as one entered the antechambers

BATTLING THE BOMBERS

of the combat station, one was impressed by a buzzing and droning of radio apparatus, alternating with the ringing of telephone bells. Experienced signals staff made contact in a few seconds with the remotest observation posts. All the cables ran to the central command table. The room was lit by indirect lighting and looked slightly eerie. Involuntarily the eye fell on bright transparent signs: Enemy Activity—Rest—Target-Spotting Practice. The air situation was shown on this board. At the present moment, the green sign "Rest" was showing. An electric clock gave the exact time. It was 01.15. Then a shrill alarm bell rang. Sleepy soldiers and intelligence airwomen poured out of the waiting rooms and hurried to their posts. All weariness vanished as soon as they heard the engines revving up on the tarmac as the young pilots were getting ready for the operation. Two hours of duty lay ahead of them and they had to be wide awake. Upon their accurate work depended the success of the ops, and perhaps the lives of these young airmen. Each soldier, each airwoman, knew the radio operators and the gunners of the individual machines only too well.

The Colonel came in full of energy. All the officers, soldiers and airwomen were at their posts. The Colonel took his place at the centre of the command table, his eyes on the large smooth panel on which now the night-fighter sectors Heron, Swan, Doe and Bear had lit up. All the cities, villages, rivers and lakes of importance were clearly defined.

"All lines clear?" the Colonel asked his Adjutant who sat next to him.

"*Jawohl*, Herr Oberst. All contacts checked. The direct lead to the fighter controller in Heron is functioning badly but we have run a jury lead over Swan."

BATTLING THE BOMBERS

"Thank you. That's fine."

There were eighty to one hundred levers on the command table. A light pressure on them sufficed to get telephonic communication over hundreds of miles. To the right of the big frosted glass panel was a board on which were posted the crews with their aircraft numbers, take-off and landing-times. On the left was a glass fluko map with indirect lighting showing the whole German territory, embracing Holland, Belgium, France and the Channel coast. On this map all enemy aircraft which had been spotted by radar sets, listening posts and reconnaissance planes were shown with their position, course and number. That evening only a few fast bombers making for Berlin reported. They were the newest type Mosquitoes, vastly superior to our night fighters.

"Zero hour minus 5—Order to all night fighter sectors. Switch on all Freya and Würzburg apparatus! Microphones ready! All lines to be branched to the command table!"

The liaison officer came in with the fighter controller. The latter went straight to the tower. An operator was already in communication with the crews in the aircraft. AS reported.

"Meteor from Thrush 36. Come in please."

"Thrush 36 from Meteor. Victor. I can hear you well. Turn down your amplifier."

"Victor—taxi to the starting point. Christmas-tree!"

This was the code word for the airfield lights to be switched on. In quick succession the controlling officer switched on the flarepath, obstacle and horizon lights and the revolving beam. From the control tower all these red, green and white lights looked like fairyland. The moonlight was so bright that one could have read a newspaper. It was a pleasure for the young pilots to take off in such weather. AS (Anton-Seigfried)—pilot Unteroffizier Zawadka—was at the starting point by the two white lamps. The fighter controller telephoned once more for the air situation. All clear! A green flare gave the signal to start. Zero, and the first machine took off, followed in quick succession by the others. The engines roared, the six-ton "crates" were under way and quickly got up speed. After a run of 800 yards the airspeed indicator showed 80 m.p.h. Stick slowly back and the machine was airborne. Zawadka kept his eyes glued to his blind-flying instruments. It was difficult to have complete confidence in these instruments and to refrain from looking outside to get one's bearings from the cloud banks or the ground. Many a young pilot had done this, stalled his aircraft and crashed into the ground from a low height. Zawadka did not make this mistake. Automatically his hand reached for the switches and took the necessary precautions. Wing flaps and undercarriage retracted. . . . The machine climbed rapidly to 1,000, to 1,500 feet.

"Thrush 36 from Meteor" rang out over the air. "Meteor from Thrush 36. Everything in order. Making for Sector Heron."

In the combat room everything was now in full swing. The sector ground stations had already reported the arrival of the night fighters and promptly gave their position in code. After decoding the position was pinpointed on the squared map and projected on to the big panel. The green dot lit up. As though attracted by a magnet, it swung slowly to the centre of the prescribed sector.

"That's gone off all right again," breathed the Colonel, with relief. "It's astonishing how quickly these airwomen out in their posts have worked. Signals seem to be in their blood."

One green dot after the other lit up on the panel. All the

BATTLING THE BOMBERS

fighters were in radio communication with the ground stations and had reached 12,000 feet.

AS flown by Unteroffizier Zawadka was on its way to the Baltic Coast. The green dot was just off the coast. The Colonel decided to make a test. A slight pressure on one of the many switches sufficed to connect him with Sector Heron.

"Put me in touch with the fighter on the ground-to-aircraft line."

"Wait a minute, the communication is disturbed by enemy transmission. We'll transfer you to another frequency."

The C.O. put on his headphones and waited for a moment. The aircraft duly reported. Calm reigned in the control room.

"Thrush 36 from Meteor. Your position directly over the coast, course 106°, altitude 13,450 feet. Out."

The fighter immediately repeated the message from control. It was a magnificent achievement on the part of signals. Meteor Headquarters was in a position to direct with great accuracy as many as thirty night fighters. This was a great relief for the crews in the air and a lightning-swift defence against strong formations of enemy aircraft. The night fighter could pursue the enemy unhindered over the Baltic, the North Sea, Holland or France, as far as the English coast. He could change course as he pleased. A brief question to Meteor and he could learn his exact position.

Even more—perhaps his machine had been badly hit in action and was not in a position to get back to the airfield on its own devices. Then the pilot sent out his S O S and control immediately began to work at feverish speed. The liaison officer took over. A glance at the panel showed him the position of the damaged machine. He then marked it on

BATTLING THE BOMBERS

the distress map which showed all airfields with their size, illumination and obstacles. Within thirty seconds with the aid of protractors, triangles and tables, he had worked out the course with all details for the nearest airfield. In another thirty seconds the ground-to-air communication, Meteor to machine in distress, was functioning.

While the machine set its course for the airfield, the controlling officer there was informed by long-distance telephone that the damaged night fighter would be landing. Beacons were switched on to show the pilot the direction of the field. Rockets rose in the air, bursting like bunches of grapes. On clear nights these radishes could be seen fifteen to twenty miles away, making it easy to spot the airfield.

Obviously when it was dark and low cloud hid the ground, when the rain beat against the windows of the aircraft and the pilot had to rely on his phosphorescent blind-flying instruments the best organised Intelligence Service in the world could not help. When gusts of wind at gale force flung the machine about the sky; when in a fraction of a second the propellers, wings and engines were swathed in thick, heavy ice, then the machine, with racing engines, risked a fatal crash into the ground. When devilish St. Elmo's fire began to dance on the aerials, cockpit panes and propellers, blinding the pilot, his eyes could not see a yard in the darkness. In these moments is born the airman who overcomes the powers of nature by his own will power. Now he must either plunge through the bad weather and crash with his crew into the teeming witches' cauldron or win through into the clear storm-free sky. Pilots trust in God far more than people would believe. With each happy landing they know that their life has been spared once more, the life they are willing to sacrifice for their country.

BATTLING THE BOMBERS

The propellers of AS threshed the icy air calmly and peacefully at 12,000 feet. Not a cloud in the sky to interfere with the visibility. Below on the dark far-off earth the rivers and lakes gleamed magnificently in the moonlight. The stars paled in the bright moonlight. Bitter cold seeped through the cannon apertures into the cockpit. The crews shivered in their fur jackets. Zawadka turned on the heating in his flying suit. The electricity warmed gloves and boots and brought some relief.

"Why doesn't the ground station answer any more?" he asked over the R.T.

"Probably a transmission fault. I'll tune in to Swan. Swan from Thrush 36—come in, please."

Swan station replied immediately. "Thrush 36 from Swan —I can hear you well. Remain on my frequency. Fighter approaching."

"We must take great care," said the gunner drily. "Otherwise there'll be some sharp shooting or he'll ram us. I'll put a red flare in the pistol in case he comes too close."

"Swan to Thrush 36—you're flying too fast. Reduce speed." Zawadka pulled back his throttle.

The result was not long delayed. Once more an angry voice called from below: "Buzzard 30! You clod! You've overshot your opponent!" Zawadka was delighted.

In actual fact he had seen his pursuer as he streaked past at great speed.

Meteor Headquarters ordered a changeover of tactics. Zawadka was now the pursuer. The controlling officer from Sector Swan reported in a horse voice: "Thrush 36— show fighter recognition signal 'Frederick'. Full throttle. Course 360. Enemy aircraft fourteen miles ahead. Altitude 13,750 feet. Out."

The engines roared. Automatically the control lamp

BATTLING THE BOMBERS

flashed the code sign F, a sign that the ground radar had picked up the night fighter and was leading him accurately to within a hundred yards of his adversary. The airspeed indicator needle rose constantly.

"Attention! Attention! Thrush 36. Enemy aircraft changing course. Course 295."

It was now quiet in the aircraft. The wireless operator switched on his SN 2. Invisibly the electric waves explored the air ahead of the aircraft, capturing everything in their path. The operator followed the pictures carefully in his cathode-ray tubes. The harsh blue glittering band flickered before his eyes. No changes appeared.

Suddenly he shouted: "I've got him!"

"You bloody clod!" grumbled the gunner. "You don't have to shout as though the machine were on fire."

Almost invisible to the untrained eye, a small zig-zag had appeared in the tubes: the adversary. Slowly it travelled to the right for the aircraft was flying on a right-hand turn. The operator now gave his "driver" a stream of measurements and led him to the target. The zig-zags appeared quite clearly in the tubes.

Now the gunner roared at the top of his voice: "I can see him—there he goes!"

Zawadka nearly jumped out of his seat at this Indian war-cry. He swore loudly. "Pull yourself together. What do you mean—there he goes? I want to know where he's flying."

"There he goes," was the reply. "Can't you see the shadow?"

Zawadka was furious, but it was no use cursing. He asked his gunner quite calmly: "Can you still see him?"

"Yes, there he goes."

"To starboard or port?"

BATTLING THE BOMBERS

"To starboard, of course. A bit higher than us."

It was by no means "of course" for Zawadka, for his eyes could see nothing but the starry sky. He banked gently to the right and gained height. Suddenly he himself roared: "I can see him. I can see him."

In his delight he let go the control column and slapped himself on the knee for this was the first aircraft he had ever seen on a night flight. The ghost-like shadow of his opponent continued to fly across the night sky and its outlines were now clearly recognisable. Zawadka could see the red-hot exhaust pipes and sparks coming from the engines. Occasionally the wings, tail unit and body were distinguishable in the moonlight. He was still eighty yards away. A short burst in, the petrol tank would have been sufficient to turn the opponent into a blazing torch. The cockpit roof glittered in the moonlight. Zawadka pressed in closer to forty and twenty yards. At last he was spotted. The other pilot switched on his position lamps and dipped his wings.

"He must have been asleep," said the radio operator; "if he flies like that in the enemy bomber stream, he'll soon be in the next world."

"Break off the operation," call the ground station. Zawadka began to lose height and set course for home.

The control from the ground is the key to the whole night-fighter defence. It sets the tasks and shows how they are to be solved. Without it, there would presumably be only a sequence of fortuitous and unconnected single combats. It is difficult to get a true conception of this fighter control. When one thinks of the vast spaces covered by night-fighter squadrons on ops, one can only compare it with the strategy used by the General Staff. And yet this is an unsatisfactory comparison for controlling, in the

BATTLING THE BOMBERS

air, has to reckon with quite different factors. To begin with the speed at which the movements of friend and foe are carried out in the combat zone. When one considers that the average speed of the bomber formations was 250 m.p.h. and that the distance between London and Berlin is only 560 miles, one soon realizes how quickly a position can change in an air battle. Two or three minutes' delay in the reports from signal services or as a result of wrong orders meant ten to fifteen miles' flight. That could be quite long enough to make a night fighter in a good position miss his enemy. It was vital to recognise at an early stage the intention of the enemy. To achieve this the individual observations from the frontiers of Europe had to reach the combat stations at lightning speed. Time also had to be allowed for checking the details. Here—also at lightning speed—they had to be decoded and translated into orders. The enemy naturally knew this and his main task therefore was to disguise his intentions as long as possible in order to hamper the defence. In addition to the actual combat, the Signals Service had to wage a bitter struggle with their apparatus. The enemy flew towards several points. He flew in zig-zags, made feint attacks and tried to jam the frequencies. All this was a great strain on the nerves. The British once maintained that 600,000 men took part in an air battle. This figure may be right or wrong, but one thing is certain—each of the men had to be not only a specialist, but also a man in perfect health.

Chapter X

THE ALLIED ARMADAS

TIRED AND SLEEPY, the crews slumped in their arm-chairs. Chess boards lay abandoned and only soft music could be heard on the wireless during the night hours. The hands of the clock wandered towards 02.00 hours. A few of the crews had retired to their bunks in full flying kit, ready at any moment to scramble. A dim red light gave a cosy tone to the room and accustomed the night-fighter pilots' eyes to the darkness. In this way the human eye needed but five minutes to adapt itself to complete darkness whereas normally the eye needs twenty minutes. Some of the men had fallen asleep with their heads on the table and one pilot was still holding the book he had been reading when he dozed off. All tension had disappeared from their features.

There was a slight crackle in the telephone. This barely audible noise roused some of them. Still half drunk with sleep, an ensign took up the receiver. His features hardened.

"*Jawohl*, Herr Oberst. Division suspects enemy mine-laying operation over the Baltic. Several reports of aircraft over the North Frisian Islands. Thank you."

In a flash the ensign's words had been grasped by the crews. It was almost incomprehensible that these words alone could have roused the deepest sleepers. All eyes were on the C.O. who was rubbing his eyes. He jumped up, got in touch with control and gave orders for three aircraft to get ready to take off. We all pored over the map eagerly discussing the chances of bringing down a mine-layer. The

BATTLING THE BOMBERS

wireless operators checked their frequencies, tables, the weather, signals and ammunition. No one as yet knew who would be sent that night over the Baltic to protect our shipping from further losses.

"It's damned late, boys," said Hauptmann Schönert, "but the Tommy is always unpredictable. I'm going to take a flip. Who's coming?"

Everyone volunteered.

"Well, Oberfähnrich Grond—you've got to be blooded sometime. Perhaps you'll be lucky tonight. Full sea rescue kit in case you're shot down over the water. Keep tuned in on the air rescue frequency. Naturally you have to help the enemy if he should fall into the drink. Any more questions?"

There was a silence.

The telephone rang shrilly. "Two crews for immediate take-off. Be careful of flakship fire."

Those who remained behind wished the hunters good luck. In the meanwhile, the C.O., Grond and their crews, made their way in the moonlight to their machines.

Schönert quickly put on a Mae West, fastened the securely packed dinghy to his parachute and checked the light flares, colour pouch, tracer ammunition, provisions and rescue flags. A slow waltz was being broadcast. The last cigarettes were being smoked when the music suddenly stopped.

"*Achtung!* Starting orders for both machines—mine-laying aircraft already over Schleswig-Holstein. Eight to twelve bombers. *Achtung! Achtung!* Take-off immediately."

Hannes Richter, the veteran wireless operator, was fiddling with his radio apparatus, convinced that he would not be of much help to the "old man" on this trip, for the mine-laying aircraft flew too low to be picked up in the

BATTLING THE BOMBERS

SN 2. But Hannes was optimistic. He could rely on the C.O.'s good scent for a scrap. A short hum of the starter and the engines started. A green lamp lit up, the Do. 217 got slowly under way, and was soon roaring down the flarepath towards the red obstacle lights. Just before reaching them it was airborne and vanished into the night.

"Everything O.K., Hannes?"

"Everything O.K., sir."

Control ordered them to Sector Heron, and then on course 300. The enemy altitude 15,000 feet. Speed 240 m.p.h. The engines droned rhythmically. Schönert had already loaded his cannon. A button pressed on the instrument panel introduced the first death-dealing shots into the barrels. Eight red lamps lit up. The time was 03.00. Lake Schwerin lay in deep sleep. In the distance a bright strip of water glittered on the horizon—the Baltic.

"*Achtung!* White Thrush! Express! Express!"

The "old man" pushed the throttle forward and the engines responded nobly. Now began the test of nerves. The white horses on the sea below looked beautiful in the moonlight, but the slightest contact with the water would smash the machine into a thousand pieces. To hit the water is more dangerous than to hit the earth. Radio communication with the Heron ground station grew clearer. Schönert gained height. Suddenly he gave a start. What was that below? Slowly and indolently something milky grey was spreading over the sea, swallowing up the gleaming surface, towering hundreds of feet above the water and steadily approaching. Fog! The machine streaked above the damp white veil. Now only the precision altimeter gave the true altitude above the water which was perhaps a few feet below the grey shroud.

BATTLING THE BOMBERS

"*Achtung* White Thrush. Enemy aircraft circling in map square X and losing height."

Hannes quickly reported the position of his machine, took his compass and set square to give his pilot the new course. Distance from the enemy, five miles. Then he removed the safety release of the SN 2. After a minute's warming-up fine, almost invisible, jagged lines appeared in the cathode-ray tubes.

"The enemy must soon appear in the gadget," said Hannes quietly.

He stared at the glittering band which was shaded on all sides in order not to dazzle the pilot. Slowly he turned the switch trying to catch the banking foe in the exploring beams.

"Go down a bit lower. Throttle back." Hauptmann Schönert obeyed.

Then a miracle of science took place. A fine small line appeared in the tube. It was the enemy mine-layer.

"He's banking," shouted Hannes in great excitement over the R.T. "Distance a mile and a half. Throttle down."

Schönert scanned the pale horizon like a lynx and did alternate aileron turns to left and right. The fog had disappeared—the best opportunity for mine-laying aircraft to drop their eggs from a low altitude. The jagged line grew larger, wandered to the left, remained stationary for a moment, wandered further left, sinking all the time.

"Enemy banking over the same spot and losing height. Probably just about to drop his mine. Distance 1,000 yards," reported Hannes.

"Switch off the radar. Keep your eyes skinned and radio silent," whispered Schönert, as though he were close enough for the Tommy to hear him.

A deathly silence on board. Head bent well forward, he

BATTLING THE BOMBERS

peered through the thick bullet-proof Perspex at the sea. The altimeter now showed 1,200 feet. The water was once more spangled in the moonlight. In the far distance the dawn was about to break. The "old man" removed the safety-catch from his guns. He had spotted the enemy, but not a word came from his lips. However, his crew knew it, for they could always tell by his face and his behaviour when he had spotted his victim. He banked sharply, lost 300 feet and suddenly a large black shadow appeared. The four-engined bomber was cruising over the Baltic, still nursing the heavy mines in its bays unaware of the danger. It spread its 120-foot wings like a bird as it lost height. The huge fuselage and the tall tail unit with the red, white and blue circles were easily recognizable. The crew of eight must have thought themselves quite safe here so far away from the coast. But at last the Tommy had spotted his pursuer, a German night fighter at 600 feet above the sea, too low to bale out. Nevertheless, the Britisher was tough. He did not give up hope. At the last moment he did a steep right-hand climbing turn, showing all his exhausts. The rear gunner fired a burst with all his guns, but Schönert was an old hand at the game and had been in this position before. At the very moment the enemy zoomed he pushed the stick forward. The tracers went over his head. He streaked at an incredible speed over the water and then zoomed. At the same moment the enormous black shape came into his sights, grew larger and a burst from eight cannons entered the fuselage, tore it open, damaged the engines and set the petrol tanks on fire. A long sinister flame trailed away below the wings of the night fighter. The crew insisted that they could feel the heat of the explosion in their cockpits. In the last second Schönert had broken off the engagement, when

BATTLING THE BOMBERS

he was perhaps no more than fifteen feet away from the flames.

He gave a sigh of relief. The giant four-engined bomber was still in the air, but the red flames were licking the engines. Soon they spread to all parts of the aircraft. This dying enemy was a gruesome sight: spellbound the crew watched the blazing Halifax which was still trailing flames like a comet. Once more the burning wings rose in the air; the blunt Perspex nose in which the pilot was still at his controls was outlined against the sky. Then it turned on its back and crashed with a monstrous explosion into the sea. A pilot's death. A sailor's death.

Upset by his opponents' courageous end, Hauptmann Schönert's voice trembled as he gave his report: "Heron from White Thrush—mine-laying aircraft shot down in Map Square X. The hunt continues."

He circled once more over the silvery waves which followed each other in all innocence, although a few seconds before they had dragged eight men down into the depths. Only a large dark patch of oil betrayed the grim combat which had taken place over the open sea under a clear moonlit sky.

The German capital with its five million inhabitants had so far been spared the mass raids. On the night of the 23rd/24th August, 1943, the R.A.F. carried their air offensive to Berlin, a distance of 560 miles.

"All crews at readiness," the order rang out over the loudspeakers on Parchim airfield. It came as a surprise. The crews rushed from their quarters and ran to their machines. Something was in the air. A bare five minutes later the whole wing was ready to take off. 23.06 hours—orders to take off! I was the first to be airborne and climbed at

BATTLING THE BOMBERS

full throttle to 15,000 feet. The night was bright and therefore in favour of the defence. In such weather at 15,000 to 18,000 feet the pilot has a field of some 350 miles. Flying over Hanover, for example, I could see the Hamburg flak in action, bombs dropping in Berlin, fires in Leipzig and incendiaries falling on Cologne. Between these cities I could see the gleaming network of flashing beacons, the dazzling searchlight cones and the square markers of night-fighter airfields. For the German night fighter, the Homeland was an open book which he had no difficulty in reading.

The ground stations reported advance enemy units over the Baltic. The Signals Service on Fehmarn Island reported strong enemy formations flying at 15,000 feet in a southwesterly direction. I knew that before each large scale raid the British agreed upon a well-known landmark as their assembly point. A glance at the map was enough to recognise this as Lake Muritz. I circled at 15,000 feet and let my SN 2 explore the air in the neighbourhood. Soon the first parachute flares fell and lit up the dark night. They swayed slowly earthwards lighting up the mirror-calm surface of the lake. The British master of ceremonies had done a good job, I thought, as I waited for the things that were bound to happen. Two more parachute flares were dropped . . . two, four, six, eight, ten—and then suddenly red tracers and flash bombs which dazzled the eye. The firework display began. Without a break the Tommies dropped flash bombs to blind the night fighters. The ground station reported the assembly of strong enemy formations north-west of Berlin. I was convinced that the raid would start from here. My fellow-pilots had also made for the marker flares and it could only be a matter of minutes before the neighbouring wings turned up at the Britisher's assembly point.

BATTLING THE BOMBERS

The British assembly, according to our experience, lasted about half an hour. Each wave had been given its exact altitude. This operation demanded the greatest discipline and self-control but was incidentally a great strain on the nerves of the British crews. But upon a perfect assembly over the agreed starting point depended the success of the raid and the lives of the crews. Not until the dispersed formations had assembled in good order did the Commodore give the order to proceed. Minute by minute, one wave after the other flew at graded altitudes towards the target. I could clearly sense the unrest in the air. Six hundred enemy bombers were circling over the lake with tons of bombs in their bays. And among them were perhaps a hundred German and fifty British long distance night fighters. Shortly before the raid the division ordered us to pursue the enemy to the capital, and to ignore their own flak, which had permission to fire as high as 24,000 feet. My crew gasped.

"This is going to be fun," said Facius, fiddling about with his SN 2.

"No need to get the wind-up," said Mahle, the gunner. "They're only firing with blanks today! Wade in, Herr Oberleutnant. If my wife, who lives in Berlin, hears that I'm in this show I shall get a proper rocket."

I let them both go on gossiping and loaded my guns. Just as I was about to go into the attack, Facius reported that his SN 2 was out of action. Now what was to be done? The only solution was to fly with the bomber stream over the city and try to spot the "furniture vans" with our naked eyes.

My comrades were already engaged with the enemy and the first bombers were going down in flames towards the lake. A wild exchange of fire was going on all round me. Tracers streaked across the sky. On the stroke of midnight the British

BATTLING THE BOMBERS

Commodore gave the signal to begin the raid by firing orange tracers. Wave after wave advanced in the direction of Berlin. I, too, flew at 18,000 feet towards the capital. Now everything was quiet and the night enfolded the city in its protective veil. And yet the storm must break loose at any moment. The city was protected by the heaviest flak batteries and the best searchlight teams. Tall flak towers hurled death and destruction at the enemy. The path of the Tommies was marked with the wreckage of burning aircraft. Forty or fifty four-engined bombers must already have paid the untimate penalty before reaching the target. And yet the performance which now started over the city defied all human description. Hell was let loose. A sea of searchlights lit up the night. Thousands of flak guns poured their lead into the air. The British Master of Ceremonies had already marked the targets with incendiaries. West and South-West Berlin were the initial targets. I could not help admiring the nerve of the path-finder who, far ahead of his stream and alone in these fireworks, carried out his task with the utmost calm, marking point by point the areas to be bombed with his incendiaries. Soon the points of attack and the quarters of the town to suffer were clearly visible to the oncoming waves. What the crews had learned in scores of raids now became the gruesome reality: carpet bombing.

Berlin defended itself magnificently. The brightly lit night was dotted with thousands of flak bursts up to 24,000 feet. I flew right into a salvo and was flung about the sky by the blast. But I got through. Right and left, above and below me, burning machines rocketed earthwards. Countless fires had sprung up below. Damaged night-fighters **fired** their distress signals, enemy bombers exploded in **the air**, spraying the city with a bright-coloured rain of gleaming confetti. A grandiose fireworks display. The constant burst-

BATTLING THE BOMBERS

ing of the flak shells tortured my nerves. The acrid stench of gunpowder entered the cockpit.

The night fighters were engaged with the enemy. Here over Berlin radar was superfluous. We could see the enemy circling over the city with our naked eyes. No one lacked a target. Red, yellow and green tracers tore through the air past my cockpit. In this inferno it was all a matter of luck for death lurked on every side. Shortly after one o'clock a four-engined Halifax crossed my path. I attacked immediately with no heed for the defence and fired at its petrol tanks. The bomber exploded and fell to earth in a host of burning fragments. 01.03. Five minutes later I saw a pair of huge shark fins just below me. I had already recognised it as my old friend the Stirling with the dangerous rear gunner. The enemy bomber grew larger in my sights and the rear gunner was sprayed by my guns and silenced just as he opened fire. The rest was merely a matter of seconds. At 01.08 this heavy bomber fell like a stone out of the sky and exploded on the ground. The nightmare came to an end.

The Britishers were on the way home. I circled over the burning city waiting for stragglers. The flak guns fell silent. Huge fires lit up the night. The crew was silent. We could not get it into our heads that our capital—Berlin—was doomed. After this battle in the heart of Germany, we all knew that the hour of victory had passed and that Hitler only wanted to gain time. But was there any sense in brooding over this? We cast a last glance at the burning city and set our course for Parchim. I landed after a flight of three hours and four minutes. My Me. 110 had received a few shell splinters but the ground staff was delighted with our success. Our wing had accounted for twenty bombers. The following day the Wehrmacht communiqué announced a terror

BATTLING THE BOMBERS

raid on Berlin and claimed 100 bombers shot down. Good—but what of the other 500? They would refuel when they got home and continue to fly until Berlin was a heap of rubble.

Raid after raid was launched against Berlin. Our wing, which had previously been well behind the line, was now in the centre of the defence zone. Night after night we sat at readiness in our machines and then when the first bombs fell on our brightly lit airfield and fast British bombers strafed our installations with cannon and machine-guns, we knew that in Germany there was now no safe rear line position. With round the clock bombing by the Allied bomber streams, the Reich itself had become a gigantic battlefield. According to a predetermined plan of attack Berlin was sinking into dust and ashes. On their nightly forays the Allies no longer needed to search for the capital, for the huge fires of the previous night were still blazing and lighting up the darkness. A blood-red glow lay over Berlin for weeks and months on end.

After these heavy raids many pilots landed at Parchim from the Dutch and Belgian zones, and among them Oberstleutnant Lent, the German night-fighter ace. As pilot in a "destroyer" group, this young airman made his first kill in the Polish campaign. In the air battle of December, 1939, over the Heligoland Bight, he accounted for three of the enemy. In 1941 Lent went over to night fighting and was successful from the start at shooting down the bombers. He became the terror of the bomber streams. Lent remained a few hours with us. In brief words, this young Group Commander described his successful combats over Berlin. His machine was refuelled and ready to take off once more. One never knew—perhaps the British would launch another raid in the early morning hours. Lent fortified himself with a glass of red wine and ate a snack. He did not even bother to take off his flying-suit to get a little rest. A quick telephone conversation with his headquarters and he learned the numbers of the enemy brought down and his own losses. Hardly had he replaced the receiver than the Chief Mechanic reported that his machine was airworthy. Lent said good-bye with a word of thanks for our hospitality and streaked away in search of new successes.

Obituary. On the 31st July, 1944, this young lieutenant-colonel was the fifteenth officer in the German forces to be awarded the Diamonds to his Knight's Cross. Two months later he was killed, undefeated by the enemy; he met an airman's death with his crew. While testing a new night fighter the port engine suddenly fell out as he banked, and Lent with his crew crashed into the ground from 150 feet.

CHAPTER XI

THE DEFENCE OF BERLIN

IN JANUARY, 1944, the Battle of Berlin reached its peak. The British used its bomber formations with intelligence. In so-called "back-handed weather," when the skies were clear over the British Isles and there was low-lying cloud at a few hundred feet over Germany, the enemy bombers took off and flew towards their targets without ever seeing the ground. This was the case on the night of the 27th January, 1944. The Met. reported a cloud ceiling of 150 feet with solid cloud up to 13,000. From 3,000 feet there was danger of icing. A fine snow fell, covering with a coat of ice the machines which started cold. There could be no lagging at the start and we had to be in the air within a minute or

BATTLING THE BOMBERS

else the engine would probably fail. The night was pitch black. Our new C.O., Hauptmann Bär, inspected the weather.

"Absolute pea-soup outside. You can't see your hand before your nose," he said as he returned to the waiting-room and detailed the crews.

Only ten out of the thirty pilots would take off if there were an alert. A landing at Parchim was out of the question. The only airfield open was Leipzig-Brandys where the ceiling was 1,500 feet. We waited anxiously, listening each hour to the report of our "Weather Frog." But there was no change. Sleet continued to fall and it was pleasant to pass the time in the warm playing a friendly game of Skat. The Allies, however, upset our calculations. Leutnant Kamprath, familiarly known as "Brinos," had been briefed that evening as radio operator to the C.O., whose own operator was on leave. Now our reservist Brinos had a wife and children. No wonder, then, that he hopped excitedly from one telephone to the other asking for the air situation. I myself had only my own skin to worry about, but I had full confidence in my machine and in my own capabilities. I made a mental note that if it came to a take-off, once my wheels were off the ground I would not look out of the machine again but rely entirely upon my blind-flying instruments. Any other course was fatal. Brinos grew calmer.

"Take it easy, the Tommy couldn't come in this muck. He's not quite tired of life yet. In this pea-soup fog, even his radar would not help him."

We consoled ourselves by agreeing, but in our heart of hearts we were far from convinced. With their latest radar apparatus, the Allies could find almost any target, even at no ceiling or with a ground mist. The picture of the landscape unwound on a special screen, as though with a film camera, before the navigator's eyes. It was a top secret.

BATTLING THE BOMBERS

The German scientists had racked their brains to discover how the British could bomb accurately through the thick cloud, until by some lucky chance they discovered this miraculous instrument in a bomber which had been shot down near Rotterdam. There was no possibility of really jamming this apparatus. An aerial photo of Berlin from 15,000 feet through a cloud bank of 9,000 feet showed clearly and in detail every street, every large square and above all the Tempelhof airfield. This new British achievement was common knowledge and that is why we were afraid of an attack that night. Only the Berliners might feel protected by the weather. What could happen? They could hardly find their own front doors with the aid of a torch.

Our C.O. was also restless and there was a certain tension in the air. If things did not happen quickly this period of waiting would be too much of a strain. My crew, Oberfeldwebel Mahle and Unteroffizier Facius, looked at me as though they wanted to say: "Well, sir, do you think you could get away with it in this weather or has the time come for us to make our wills?" Since I could not bear this mood I ordered my crew to get into the machine and await further developments. Poldi Fellerer, No. 5 Squadron Leader, followed suit.

"Where are you off to?" asked the C.O. as we left the hut.

Poldi replied that we would get accustomed to the darkness in our aircraft and warm up the instruments.

The mechanics in their huts were quite amazed when they heard our decision.

"You're not thinking of taking off in this are you, sir? Even the Chief's left his bicycle at home and has come on foot."

BATTLING THE BOMBERS

We had to laugh as we climbed into the cockpit. I switched on all my instruments and gave them a thorough check-up. Facius fiddled with his apparatus and tuned in to the notorious Calais station. The sugary-sweet music was suddenly interrupted by the well-known V-sign and we heard the announcer say: "Berlin, you were once the most beautiful city in the world. Berlin, look out for eleven o'clock tonight!" We were dumbfounded. I rushed to the telephone and got put through to the C.O.

"The Calais radio has just warned its friends of a raid tonight about eleven o'clock."

The whole squadron repaired to their machines. The clock on my instrument panel showed 20.00 hours. At this moment a green flare was fired from the control tower. Starting orders at last! The C.O.'s machine stood next to mine. I can still see Hauptmann Bär busy at work in the half-dark machine while Brinos checked his contact with the other crews on the R.T. Everyone answered. Brinos ended with: "Well, happy landings, all."

I was all set to take off but it was a point of honour that the C.O. should take off first. I taxied close behind him to the start. Visibility was appalling and the green flarepath lights could hardly be seen through the thick rain lashed Perspex.

The C.O. took off. The engines roared and a dense rain of sparks swirled in the slip-stream behind him. He had hardly left the runway than I gave my machine full throttle and streaked after him. All my nerves were concentrated on this take-off. I soon got up speed, pulled her off the ground and retracted my undercarriage. Just as I was about to retract my wing flaps a terrible explosion shook my machine and a scarlet flame pierced the night. I was half-dead with fright. For a second I thought that my machine had crashed but nothing could have happened for the altimeter showed 90 feet and I was in level flight.

Then the truth struck me in a flash: Hauptmann Bär had crashed. I stared grimly at my instruments and gained height. Now I must on no account let my mind wander. At 3,000 feet the propellers and the leading edges of the wings began to ice up. I realized this at once from the irregular running of the engines. Mahle lit up the wings with his torch: there was already a thick coating of ice. We were now at a dangerous height in which the temperature outside was about zero and the sleet was turning to ice on the undercooled machine.

Everything happened at lightning speed. As a precaution I told the crew to check their parachutes and to bale out as soon as I gave the orders. The machine grew heavier and the controls answered more slowly each moment. I now had to decide whether I should take her down into a warmer belt of air or hold on and try to fly through the danger zone. To lose height would in practice mean the end of the operation and furthermore entail the danger that, with any further icing, we should be too low to bale out. I therefore decided to go on climbing and to wait and see whether the machine would make the grade or not.

The engines were running at full throttle. Thick ice splinters broke off with loud reports and thumped against the nose.

Mahle reported: "Herr Oberleutnant—it's pointless. The tail unit's beginning to ice up. The temperature outside is now 4° below."

I noticed that my joy-stick was no longer answering. Fortunately the trimming wheel was still working. I set the machine at tail-heavy, and pushed the throttle home to its utmost limit. The engines could rev like this for five minutes at the utmost. But why should I spare the engines when it was a question of the crew's life. I remembered the English bomber formation which, in the winter of 1943, iced up over the North Sea and, as a last resort, jettisoned bombs, equipment and petrol in the sea to lighten the machines. And yet they could not reach the safety height, and more than forty four-engined bombers crashed like gigantic lumps of ice into the icy waters. No rescue was possible. Would the same thing happen to me? Our last chance was to bale out. But it was not very pleasant in this sort of weather to jump into the unknown. So I must go on climbing, climbing, climbing. All eyes were riveted on the wings. The machine was almost on stalling point but at last we were out of danger. The layer of ice gradually broke off. My good old Me. 110 was now climbing faster and the temperature outside sank to 15° below. The danger of icing was past. But there still remained the darkness and the impenetrable cloud bank around us. The altimeter showed 6,000 feet, but not until 12,000 did we catch a glimpse of the stars. God be praised—we had won through. Now, above us, was a cloudless sky with bright stars such as one only sees on clear winter nights. I skimmed the clouds, heading for the Baltic coast and waited for further orders. I almost felt like patting my Me. 110 as though she had been a human being.

I wondered what could have happened to Hauptmann Bär and his crew. How could he have crashed? I thought of Kamprath and his family. They could not have got away with it for they could not have been at more than 200 feet. This was far too low to bale out.

My thoughts were interrupted by an order from the ground station: "White Angus from Meteor—*Achtung, Ach-*

BATTLING THE BOMBERS

tung! Strong bomber formation at 15,000 feet over the Baltic flying on a south-westerly course."

Above Wismar my radio operator caught the first enemy machine in his SN 2. The magic began. At 20.36 the first enemy bomber was brought down and spun through the clouds after my first burst. Twenty minutes later, a second crashed just outside the capital. The British drew a square above the clouds with their parachute flares. We could see nothing of the city below. Thousands of flak bursts confirmed our arrival over the target. Wave after wave of bombers flew across the square of light and dropped their loads within this area, through the cloud on to the city.

I approached this square on a southerly course and spotted a couple of four-engined Lancasters directly above the target. After a short attack the first bomber exploded and fell in burning debris through the clouds. The second banked steeply to starboard, trying to escape. The Tommies fired at me with all their guns, framing my aircraft with gleaming tracers. I pressed home the attack; the tail unit grew ever larger in my sights. Now was the time to shoot. The fire power of my guns was terrific. My armour-piercing shells riddled the well-protected wing tanks and the pilot's armoured cockpit; the tracers set fire to the petrol and the H.E. shells tore great holes in the wings. It was no wonder that my fourth bomber that night crashed in flames

I was all in. Four kills in forty-five minutes were too much for the nerves. The raid was over and the enemy bombers were on their way back to England, protected by the cloud bank. I circled for about ten minutes to calm down. Only then did I begin to think: now, where am I to land? The ground stations continued to give the weather reports. There were nearly forty night fighters in the air, all anxious to see terra-firma once more. The weather report was calamitous.

BATTLING THE BOMBERS

Nearly all the airfields reported a ceiling of 150 feet, bad visibility and snow storms. What was to be done? My crew was sitting there half-frozen.

"Go through that again Herr Oberleutnant?" said Mahle. "No, it's better to get above Parchim and fall out of the sky like Father Christmas."

I could not countenance this suggestion to abandon my machine. Since Leipzig-Brandys had reported that the clouds were now at 240 feet and nearly all the machines would be landing there, I decided to fly back to Parchim. There I knew every hillock, every tree and every house. My crew was exhausted and silent. This disturbed me. I flew for thirty minutes above the cloud at 15,000 feet and reached our home field. I got into communication with control. The familiar voice of the controlling officer replied. At first he wanted to know some details of our kills. He's worried, I thought. He's standing with both feet on the ground while we still don't know whether we can make a safe landing. But I could understand his curiosity for even a "kiwi" gets excited by the success of his pals after sitting alone all night at his post.

"Four," I replied.

"Victor, Victor. Message received," he replied. "One, two, three, four—shot down. Congratulations. Take great care on landing. Ceiling 150 feet—snow has ceased. Am putting out the shroud and firing radishes. Reception good."

So down we went into the muck. Putting out the shroud meant pointing the ground searchlight vertically to light up the clouds. At 450 feet over the airfield I should have to spot this searchlight. Slowly we circled round the beacon losing height. At 4,500 feet, the machine started to ice up again. To get out of the danger quickly I throttled back and dived sharply to 1,500 feet. It worked. The icing ceased. But now came the ticklish point—the landing. We were now losing height at three feet per second, feeling our way carefully through the clouds, constantly losing height. It was still pitch dark around us. Then suddenly I saw lights flash. They could only be the radishes. And a moment later the shroud appeared. So we were directly above the airfield. In a flat turn I got into position to land and switched over to the Barque approach position. The Ultra Short Wave Barque approach was still the safest way of landing blind. To port of the flying-in course echoed dots and to starboard dashes. If we were on the right course I should hear a sustained burr in the headphones and moreover control lamps went on. Taking into consideration the wind conditions I was now flying in the region of the sustained tone towards the airfield. About a mile and a half away from the field I lowered my undercarriage and wing flaps and came down to 150 feet. My run-in was good.

The controlling officer reported for the last time. "Your course correct—you can land."

I confirmed the report and told him to turn off the searchlight. Throttled back to stalling point, we approached the airfield and now no lights were visible. Then the warning signal rang out "Pip-pip-pip-pip." So I was 1,500 yards from the runway. I set the wing flaps at 70° and kept at an approach speed of 100 m.p.h. This flight position was very dangerous and mobile; if I missed the runway it would be fatal. Finally I saw blurred lights on the horizon and the signal rang out "Da-da-da-da". Now we were 300 yards from the airfield. At that moment I recognised the flarepath and put the machine down at far too great a speed. I did not think we should ever stop. Touched down at last and taxied towards the red end-field lights. I braked like a maniac and pulled up just on the edge of the open country.

BATTLING THE BOMBERS

I said a little prayer now that I was down again. Mahle pulled open the cockpit and we could all breathe the cool night air.

The mechanics were all delighted. They were always proud of their machines and their crews, but news of the death of Hauptmann Bär and his gunner damped the joy of the other crews who had been on ops.

"And what about Leutnant Kamprath?" I asked.

"Can you imagine it?" was the reply. "He baled out from 240 feet. What a bit of luck. Hardly had the parachute opened than he hit the ground. It was a matter of about ten seconds. He's already recovered."

"What a crazy business," I replied, as I hurried over to the ops room.

Brinos was already in a happy state of mind. On the one side joy, and on the other side grief. But we had grown hard in this pitiless war. Hauptmann Bär was dead and he was not our only casualty. Leutnant Sorko and Oberfeldwebel Krammerer had been shot down with their crews and were dead. After bad icing, Leutnant Spoden baled out with his crew and landed successfully.

On landing he had a little misadventure and his account made us all roar with laughter. Spoden told it in the following words: "My crate grew heavier and heavier. Thick lumps of ice formed on the wings and the screws. 'I'm no flying refrigerator,' I said to my mates and showed them a little break in the clouds. It had come to that. The aircraft was out of action and I thought we'd better bale out. At first my crew wouldn't hear of it, so I said: 'Well, boys, if you don't want to, I bid you all good night. Peter's jumping.' You can imagine how fast they were! Houp-la No. 1 . . . Houp-la No. 2 . . . and I followed them.

"It was as cold as in Siberia and I remember thinking

that it was a good thing I had put on mother's warm, woollen socks. Well, how shall I describe what happened then? It was as dark as in the jungle and I had a feeling that I should soon be down. You wouldn't credit it. My descent lasted an eternity. Suddenly there was a jerk as if someone had put on the brake and I was left hanging and swinging in the air. My parachute had got caught up in a tree. At first I was pleased that I had got down safely, but unfortunately there was no one to tell me how far I was from the ground. I'd lost my torch as I'd baled out, of course. I was scared stiff to slip out of the lift-webs and jump down. Then I found my knife in my left pocket. I took it out, let it fall, and listened. Flop! It could have been six but it could have been thirty feet. I had no confidence in this test and waited for dawn.

"It was amusing at first, swinging about in the tree, but it soon palled. My limbs grew as stiff as pokers. I prayed that it would grow light but nothing happened. So I hung on my belt and waited longingly for the first light of day. As soon as dawn broke I woke up from a doze and looked at the ground. My eyes nearly started out of my head. Hardly three feet below me was a wonderfully soft forest floor." That was the end of Peter's story. We roared with laughter and Peter's tree landing went the rounds of the whole Night Fighter Arm.

Chapter XII

AIR ACROBAT

SHORTLY AFTER this Peter Spoden and Leutnant Knieling were both in the Parchim hospital. The two men had been

BATTLING THE BOMBERS

wounded in a night combat. I visited them one Sunday morning just as the chief doctor was making his rounds. I had to wait a little. As a result of the strangely peaceful atmosphere in the hospital, I grew thoughtful and stared out of the window up at the blue sky. The contrast between day and night is fantastic. Hardly twelve hours ago it was once more an inferno over Berlin. Twelve hundred Allied bombers attacked in wave after wave, pouring burning phosphorus to relight the fires which had been extinguished in the grievously wounded capital. That night of the 15th–16th February, 1944, I shot down my thirteenth, fourteenth and fifteenth opponents.

But what did fifteen four-engined bombers shot down mean? An individual success, that was all. With the destruction of Berlin the crisis of the Nazi dictatorship began, for this round-the-clock bombing exhausted the civilian population. Even those who had firmly believed in victory began to doubt. What a contrast between the events of the previous night and the peace reigning here in Parchim. The patients were reading the accounts of the terror attacks on Berlin in the papers, but who could have any conception of the extent of these attacks? I myself could not grasp it or that a proud initial success had become a bitter struggle to preserve the fatherland.

My thoughts were interrupted by a sister who told me with a smile that I could visit my friends. Knieling lay pale and apathetic in his bed. The poor fellow had a bullet through his thigh. With his last strength, he had managed to land before fainting from loss of blood. Now he was on the way to recovery. Our indestructible Spoden was wreathed in smiles. He wanted to get out of the hospital and fly again. But the house surgeon would not hear of it and informed me that Spoden would be released as unfit for flying. Peter winked at me when he heard this. As soon as we were alone, he hopped out of bed and fetched a bottle of brandy which his orderly had hidden in his locker.

"Prosit! See you soon again with the squadron! When I'm out of here, you know what the quack can do. Do you suppose I'm going to stay on the ground while all this is going on?"

I promised Spoden that I would fetch him as soon as possible and let him keep his hand in on a joy ride over Denmark.

The promise was soon fulfilled. Peter reported gaily from hospital and on the following day I took him up. I borrowed a two-seater Focke-Wulf 184 from the "old junk shop" in our air-park. Brinos acted as wireless operator and Peter was stowed away in the luggage hold. To avoid any danger we hedge-hopped over Lake Schwerin, the Baltic and the Little Belt to the Danish airfield Aalborg.

Denmark, despite five years of war, was still a land of milk and honey. It would do no harm to stock up our private larders. At 12.50 hours we landed at Aalborg. Brinos took our papers to the Base Commandant and drew the necessary kroner. He soon came back beaming. A glance at his full notecase and we drove in an Opel in high spirits to the town. We ordered cream tarts in a pretty little café. Since we had not eaten such a thing for a long time and they were likely to upset our stomachs, we washed them down with plenty of brandy.

At the next table two pretty girls were obviously amused at our appetites and seemed friendly enough. Peter went over to the attack. Who could blame him? The two girls were soon sitting at our table and found him extremely amusing. An appointment was soon fixed for a round of the dance halls and bars that evening. Peter was in such good

BATTLING THE BOMBERS

form that he would have liked to remain a few days in Aalborg. The following morning at breakfast, all suffering from thick heads, we realised that we had bought nothing for our larder in Parchim. Brinos counted our communal wealth. We still had plenty of kroner left. Armed with two kit-bags we visited the shops. Within two hours they were full of ham, bacon, chocolate, coffee, schnapps, cigarettes and jam.

But we still had some money left. What was to be done? We fetched our Opel and drove to the airfield where we found a canteen. As we entered we noticed a gigantic ham hanging from the roof. Peter immediately went over to the barman and asked what the "bear's arse" cost. The man goggled at us and could not believe that we really wanted to buy the whole ham which must have weighed a hundredweight. But Brinos planked our last kroner down on the table and we were allowed to carry off our booty. But what were we to do with all our purchases? The good old Focke-Wulf had hardly room for three people and certainly not for three kit-bags full of food. But we had to manage somehow. At 18.00 hours, when we took off, Peter was lying with a bottle of cognac in the luggage hold hugging his "bear's arse". He could not put on his parachute for there was no room.

"What's the use?" said Peter. "If we fall in the drink the bacon will surface and I shan't let go of it."

At 20.00 hours we landed with our valuable food reserves in Parchim. We were received with as much excitement as though we had been the Pied Piper of Hamelin. Wherever there is bacon there are always rats!

A few days later Peter came in the evening to the ops room and asked permission to fly. The C.O. shook his head and Peter retired with a resigned air. At 21.00 hours,

BATTLING THE BOMBERS

readiness was ordered and a few moments later all the machines were airborne. As we left the pens I recognised, in the searchlight beam, Peter and his radio operator, hovering round the machines. I suspected nothing and took off. Only when I was on my way to Berlin did I think: I wonder if Peter's done anything off his own bat. He's not fit to fly yet and if the C.O. says no he must accept the fact. The Tommies came over that night in good, fine weather. The operation seemed to promise success for both the attack and the defence. Already on the approach flight the bombers were brought down out of the sky like ripe fruits. Over Berlin the defence was at its peak and 120 out of the 800 bombers did not return home. Sweating profusely after three hours flying, I landed at Parchim after streaking across the airfield dipping my wings as a sign of victory. There was great excitement at Headquarters. All the crews had reported kills and there were no casualties. The interrogations lasted interminably.

Then Control tower suddenly called, asking if anyone knew details of C9-HN which had not returned. No one knew. This aircraft belonged to my squadron and was posted on the board as reserve machine. I called up the Chief Mechanic and asked what had happened to it. The N.C.O. had taken off about twenty minutes after the others in the reserve machine. A fine surprise! The C.O. was furious although in his heart he did not take Peter's insubordination amiss. The Intelligence apparatus started to function and within half an hour we had news. Spoden had not landed. He could no longer be in the air for his fuel could not have lasted for more than three and a half hours. The C.O.'s anger vanished at this news, for he had a soft spot in his heart for Peter.

BATTLING THE BOMBERS

What had happened to him? At this juncture Flak Headquarters, Berlin, came on the line.

The C.O. hurried to the telephone and kept stammering "*Jawohl*, Herr Oberst." His face grew longer. Slowly he put down the receiver. "Spoden has been shot down right over the city. The Searchlight Battery had caught an enemy bomber in its cone at 17,000 feet when a night fighter suddenly attacked it. The Britisher replied to its fire and within a matter of seconds both machines spun down earthwards on fire. The searchlight battery lit up the two machines down to 4,500 feet and as they crashed noticed a man hanging on to the tail unit. That could only have been Spoden. As a result of his wound, he no longer had the strength to tear himself free from the machine. Well, that's it boys. He's paid for his obstinacy with his life."

The moon was low. I could not believe it and kept thinking of our flight with the giant ham over the Baltic. That simply can't happen to Peter, I thought. The Good Lord will get him out of it somehow. Brinos agreed with me. We sat in our armchairs and waited for some real news one way or the other. At five o'clock in the morning the telephone rang. It was Berlin Flak Division again. I seized the phone and breathed a sigh of relief. Spoden was badly wounded in hospital. His life was not in danger. His crew had all baled out and landed successfully.

Peter was brought back to Parchim on the following day. His bed in the hospital was still vacant. The house surgeon cursed him roundly but immediately started to treat him.

A few days later, when Peter was in a condition to speak, we heard his story: "When you'd all taken off I felt terribly lonely. Making up my mind, I ordered the Oberfeldwebel to get the reserve machine ready to take-off. He hesitated

BATTLING THE BOMBERS

but I pointed out that in wartime orders were orders and that I was now giving one. He obeyed me. It was over Berlin. I had put up some competition to the flak and shot down two Lancasters in the searchlight cones. I thought to myself: the main thing is to bring them down. Then the third one came into the beam—a Short Stirling. You know —as big as a barn door with four engines. I attacked, and as I broke away noticed that my machine had been hit in the fuselage. Flames were coming out on both sides. I could get no reply from the radio operator. I gave the order to bale out but he had already gone. Both his cockpit roof and mine had flown away.

"When I tried to get out something caught me fast by the leg. Half-way out of the cockpit I had to return and tear something off. The flames were already licking my parachute. Well—Prosit! Bad hats always seem to come through. My aircraft was spinning like a merry-go-round. Somehow I got out at 15,000 feet. I was more flung out than anything and crashed against the tail unit. I noticed that I was in a searchlight beam. The wind held me pressed against the tail. I waved my arms and legs and could not shake free either up or down. And the descent went on. Finally the machine spun in the opposite direction and I was flung out to the rear.

"Now keep cool, I said to myself. Count twenty to twenty-five and then pull the rip-cord. It turned with me on the end and one of the lines was torn. The fire, you know. . . . Then I fell through smoke and flame and passed out. When I woke up I lay in a street between blazing houses. The flak was still firing. I was carried into a cellar and given some brandy. Someone had been sweating with anxiety—the officer of the searchlight battery. He visited me next day in hospital. I learned from him that I only broke free at about 5,000 feet. He thought that he was helping me by lighting me up!"

CHAPTER XIII

THE JET FIGHTER

WHILE the Battle of Berlin continued with undiminished fury, smaller R.A.F. formations raided the other German cities. In this way the enemy split the German defence and constantly set the German Night-Fighter Command a problem as to which was the main attack. At the beginning of March, 1944, a medium-sized British formation appeared over France heading for Southern Germany. We were in our ops room following the progress of the bombers on the map. Our C.O. asked Divisional Headquarters for permission to take off. The Division hesitated because it feared a simultaneous attack on Berlin. In this way valuable minutes were lost. In the meantime the leading formations had reached the Franco-German frontier in the Hagenau region. We now received orders to take off for Southern Germany. It was already 02.00 hours when the last machines from Parchim streaked down the flarepath and set a southerly course. At 15,000 feet over the Thuringia Forest the directing officer reported the first bombs on Stuttgart. The clock on my instrument panel showed 02.59 hours. Thus we still had forty-five minutes flying time before we reached the Swabian capital. By the time we reached Stuttgart the British bombers had left and huge fires bore witness to their work of destruction.

BATTLING THE BOMBERS

Pursuit was pointless, for once the British bombers had dropped their load and were on the return journey they were as fast as the German night fighters. This was not surprising for we had been flying the same crates since 1940. Four years previously I had learned night flying over Stuttgart in an Me. 110, Berta series. At the time it was a reasonably fast and handy "destroyer" aircraft. That day I was circling in the same machine, Gustave series, over burning Stuttgart. Our night-fighter machines had not grown any faster but rather slower. So we flew back to Parchim without success after wasting thousands of gallons of costly petrol. On the return flight the ground station gave us details of the night attack. Four hundred bombers had flown over Stuttgart and dropped an incredible tonnage of phosphorus, high explosive and incendiary bombs on the city.

In the spring of 1944 the R.A.F.'s night attacks on the capital ceased. For the moment the great destruction had come to an end. Everything in the nature of war factory had been razed in daylight raids carried out by American Boeings. My night-fighter wing had come out of the Berlin battle with flying colours. Within six months we had shot down an entire group of four-engined Halifaxes, Stirlings and Lancasters, in other words about 100 bombers with the 800 members of their crews. Our own losses were pitiful. In these air battles the following pilots and their crews met their deaths. Hauptmann Bär, Hauptmann Schurbel, Oberleutnant Sorko, Leutnant Metz, Overfeldwebel Kammerer, Unteroffizier Horget and Unteroffizier Zawadka. A further two crews went down in flames and were seriously wounded. Thus a complete night-fighter squadron was lost in these combats over Berlin. After a few days' rest and convalescence, during which our wing was reinforced by young crews, we received orders to leave for Leipheim on the Danube. The uncertainty and panic in the war leadership was now having its effect on the operational pilots. Hardly had we set foot in Leipheim and got things in order than we were ordered to Kitzingen. We packed our things and took off. We arrived in Kitzingen just before dusk like a swarm of locusts. Our crews brought a breath of fresh air into the peaceful training school atmosphere reigning there. Hardly had we got warm than new orders came through: "Return to Leipheim," and the muddle continued. "Report at once to Hagenau in Alsace!"

Our General Staff could certainly think quicker than we flew, for on the following day we were ordered back to Leipheim. However, it was good practice and gave our machines no time to get rusty. Finally it seemed as though we were to remain at Leipheim.

On this airfield, a branch of the Messerschmitt factory was still working, building jets. This new invention was of the greatest interest to us. The test pilots set out daily with great explosions along the runway, disappeared on the horizon and in a few moments reappeared flying at 500 m.p.h. over the field. A gentle whistle in the distance, a terrific roar and they were gone. The landings seemed breakneck and dangerous. The normal starting and landing runway for jet fighters should be at least 2,000 yards. The concrete runway in Leipheim was only 900. Thus every landing was a risk for both pilot and machine. Nevertheless I found them most impressive.

One day I drove over to the works to have a look at this wonder machine. I noticed that the Me. 262 had two engines but no propellers. Furthermore inside the engine casings were two turbines which caused a propulsion behind which it was inadvisable to stand. The flames that spurted from the turbine chambers commanded respect. I

BATTLING THE BOMBERS

thought that any moment such an apparatus would explode, but I was obviously wrong for the test pilots sat unperturbed in their cockpits and seemed to delight in these fireworks.

I was very curious and asked the works manager for an explanation of the machine.

That all seems quite simple, I thought, when he had finished his lecture. The first step was to press a button and a small petrol engine began to purr quite harmlessly. This engine drove the turbines. When the requisite revs had been reached the pilot injected J2, a weak distillate, into the petrol flow. This J2 reached the compressed heated air of the combustion chambers and ignited of its own accord. Sparking plugs were therefore superfluous. The turbine revs rose from 4,000 to 5,000 r.p.m. Another few drops of J2 and the crate hurtled off at 550 m.p.h. In the air the rev counter and the temperature had to be watched. Temperatures of over 800° in the combustion chamber could be dangerous and it was then prudent to reduce the intake. By and large it was a fine job. Duration of flight: 25 minutes. This bird could reach 18,000 to 21,000 feet within a minute. In a dive it was twice as fast.

"Why don't you get in and have a look at her from inside," said the works manager.

Without a thought I swung myself into the pilot's seat. At that moment I had not the slightest intenion of flying, for I found the whole machine too weird. Gradually I grew accustomed to the whine of the turbines and the long trail of fire which came out of the "onion." This onion was at the rear of the turbine and served the same purpose as the muter on a jazz trumpet. When it closed up the hole the air could not get out. The compressed air in a trumpet produces a very clear tone but in a jet fighter it gives enormous forward propulsion. If the onion is opened the

BATTLING THE BOMBERS

air can escape and the recoil is diminished. In the case of a trumpet this results in a dull tone. When the plane's turbines are running on the ground the onion is wide open. From the cockpit I gave no more throttle than with a piston engine: I merely had to open and close the onion. I gradually realised that this turbo-jet had great advantages over an ordinary piston engine. The turbines needed no warming up and the machine was ready to take off as soon as the self-starter was used. Moreover there could be no sparking plug or cooling troubles; whereas flying with full throttle was forbidden in all piston engined aircraft, it was normal in this new type. My fingers itched and, as a veteran, I felt ashamed to get out of the machine without taking her up for a flip.

The works manager uttered his views. "The country still needs you as a night fighter and I'm afraid I've left my flying suit in Augsburg, Herr Oberleutnant."

I had the chocks removed and closed the cockpit roof. The works manager jumped down from the wing. I had made up my mind. At the worst, if I got into trouble, I could use the catapult release and bale out. That must be quite a pleasure in daylight. One machine more or less did not matter very much now to the Luftwaffe. A swift glance at the instrument panel and I was streaking along the runway with the onion closed; in a matter of seconds I was approaching the end of the airfield, I pulled her off the ground at 160 m.p.h. It was too soon and the machine sank until she was barely off the ground. Once more my luck held good. Another few yards and I should have been in the soup. At 240 m.p.h. I retracted my wing flaps. Now there was no more holding her. The air speed indicator rose in a few seconds to 300, 360, 420, 520 m.p.h. This was fast enough for me. I carefully opened the onion because of

BATTLING THE BOMBERS

the high temperature. I was still not quite at my ease with the combustion chambers. At 1,500 feet I swept over Ulm and did a steep left hand climbing turn as I arrived over the cathedral. It was not a climb: I was fairly shot into the blue sky. The cathedral grew smaller and smaller until it was a mere toy below and my altimeter showed 15,000 feet. I'd like to run into a few Tommies now, I thought. It would be a pleasure. I looked upon this machine now as the eighth wonder of the world, and in my enthusiasm I dived and zoomed like a rocket, flinging her about all over the sky.

Leipheim was now just below me. In a power dive I pulled out just above the sheds and buildings and roared across the airfield at over 600 m.p.h. This was strictly forbidden, but I could not have cared less. Suddenly I realised that I must get this miracle down on the ground, for I had been flying nearly twenty-five minutes. I took this landing very seriously. In a broad sweep I reached Gunzburg at the prescribed height of 900 feet for a landing speed of 220 m.p.h. Slowly I lowered the undercarriage and wing flaps and put her nose into the wind. By the grace of God there was a fairly stiff breeze which made landing easier. The speed decreased. At 200 m.p.h. the crate was at stalling point but I held her at this speed and glided down to within 100 yards of the white cross-line. My speed sank to 150. The wheels touched the ground at the very edge of the airfield, and once more I was rushing along the runway. This time I had to pull up before I reached the end of the field or else I should come to a sticky end. I pressed with all my strength on the brake pedals. They answered. I suddenly had complete confidence in this machine and was delighted with my first solo on jets. But by night I preferred my slow

BATTLING THE BOMBERS

old Me. 110, so the onion by day and the throttle lever by night.

The following midday I was sitting peacefully in Brinos' room celebrating his birthday with a cup of coffee. His wife had come to pay him a visit. No wonder the coffee and cakes tasted so good. Our C.O., Hauptmann Fellerer, was away on duty and I was in charge of the wing. The Adjutant, Walter, reported a big formation of American bombers flying towards southern Germany.

"Most unsporting of them to disturb us at our coffee," said Brinos, consoling his wife. But Frau Kamprath suddenly grew nervous and opened the window. In the distance we could hear the sinister familiar drone: this made Brinos nervous too.

"Mami," he said, "put your things on, take your suitcase and cross the Danube to be on the safe side."

His wife hastily left the house while Brinos followed me to the dispersal pens. The machines were camouflaged. The whole ground staff had left the eyrie according to orders. The drone grew louder and a glance to the west showed us that the bomber stream was flying on a direct course for Leipheim.

"Get in the car," I shouted and jumped in myself. I pressed the self-starter but nothing happened. The batteries were down. We were standing between the machines. It was a ticklish position. I looked round for the best chance of getting clear of the carpet bombing.

"Come on, Brinos, to the other side of the autobahn. There are no sheds or machines there."

We were soon running for our lives. But we were too late. We were still half-way across the runway when the leading American machines dropped the aimer. It fell in the field to the east of the runway.

BATTLING THE BOMBERS

"Lie down," I roared to Brinos, and we crouched in the grass.

A thunderstorm broke over our heads and at each moment the whistle of bombs would begin. But nothing happened. Once more our luck had held.

"Come on," I roared, "they're making another circuit. Their run in wasn't good enough."

The next wave was about two miles from the field, followed by others. We had to get out of this within a couple of minutes or else we should be dead meat. Brinos ran with his short legs and I followed him with my long ones.

The formation was now over the field. This time the marker bomb fell into the Messerschmitt Works Production shed and there was a sinister rustle and whistling in the air. Like old soldiers we lay in a ditch at the edge of the field with our heads buried in the ground. Crump, crump! A deafening explosion and within a few seconds the pilots' eyrie was shrouded in a giant cloud of smoke. The Americans attacked in ten waves. At each wave we slipped deeper into our watery ditch.

"Better be dripping wet and alive than dry and dead," said Brinos.

We thought that the bombs must have fallen very close to us for the earth rocked. During a lull I looked over to the airfield buildings and sheds. They were a blazing heap of ruins. The runway was still untouched. Then another wave flew directly in our direction.

"It's the runway this time, Brinos. Let's hope they aim well, or we've had it."

The bombs whistled down. As in our happy days of infantry training we now lay flat in the ditch with our noses just out of the water. Deafening explosions as the runway was hit. Bits of concrete fell round our unprotected backsides. It would be all over if we got one of them on the head. I remembered the steel helmet which had lain for years unused and dusty inside my locker. I could have used it now, but we pilots always had a prejudice against steel helmets, gas masks, rifles and hand grenades. So all I could do now was to think nostalgically of my steel helmet and protect the back of my head with my hands. The danger was soon over. We got out of our ditch like drowned dogs and laughed with glee. But our laughter was short lived when we saw the mess that the Yankees had made. The sheds and buildings were ablaze and hours later delayed action bombs kept exploding. The wrecks of about sixty jet aircraft lay there. The following day we packed up all we could rescue and left for Hagenau in Alsace. The crews travelled by train in all directions to fetch new aircraft. Two days later our wing commander could report that we were ready for action.

Chapter XIV

SWISS INTERLUDE

On the evening of April 28th, 1944, a mild spring breeze was blowing over Hagenau airfield. Was it the spring or our new surroundings which made us feel so relaxed? In any case the crews were in splendid fettle. It may of course have been due to the little town of Hagenau itself. After an afternoon trip through our new garrison we could all feel the French atmosphere. Everything was different, more lighthearted and charming. Each of us felt that something was in the air and in this mood we met for our briefing at 21.00 hours in the ops room. The C.O., too, was in a spring mood. I had rarely attended such a calm briefing as on that evening. It was as though we had all drunk champagne. One would have thought that a feast was being prepared at the headquarters of No. 3 Squadron, No. 6 Night-Fighter Wing, instead of a serious night's ops. Actually we did not expect to be sent on a mission for the weather was too fine. At 6,000 feet a few clusters of cloud stood in the night sky through which the moon cast its silvery light. This weather was far too unfavourable for the Tommies and we began to make our plans for a night off. Our adjutant had found a nice little *boîte de nuit* in Hagenau with music, sweet wine and everything else that a night fighter could need. Rendezvous 02.00 hours. It was late, but not too late, and at the moment it was only 22.00 hours. What was the old saying—"So much can happen on a wonderful night in May?"

Outside on the airfield stood the brand-new machine which I had fetched from the Parchim sheds: my C9. ES, fitted with all modern comforts and refinements. Outwardly she looked a trifle virginal for she was painted white from nose to tail; but the cannon muzzles looked far from innocent. Her new equipment included the Naxos apparatus, a greatly improved radar eye. If a British night fighter tried to creep up from behind in the pitch darkness this apparatus lit up and gave due warning when he was 500 yards away. A quick change of course and the pursuing Tommy had someone on his tail. In addition to this an electric altimeter—also a fine invention. The radar was now first class. It invariably picked up the bomber at 6,000 yards and led the fighter on an "Ariadne's thread" to its prey. And finally the armament: in front were two cannon and four machine-guns, with a further two cannon pointing upwards, an innovation successfully introduced by my crews and now mass produced by the Messerschmitt works. I was really proud of my C9. ES and felt rather sorry that presumably I should not have an opportunity of putting her though her paces that night.

Ten minutes passed. At about 00.30 hours we were preparing to go off on our party Chez Yvonne. No one thought of sleep. That night Brinos, our Intelligence Officer, was briefed as my wireless operator because my regular sparker, Grasshoff, was away on four days' leave. Brinos sat with my gunner, Oberfeldwebel Mahle, in a cosy corner.

Ten minutes later orders came through: "All machines take off for the Nancy sector. A British bomber formation is approaching, making for Southern Germany."

"What a pity. I was looking forward to going Chez Yvonne," I said to the crew.

"Never mind," said Kamprath, "tonight I shall be in at my first kill."

Mahle said nothing and busied himself as usual with his cannon and machine gun. He had superstitiously placed my officer's cap on the ammunition drum. At 00.48 hours we took off into a south-west wind for Nancy. At 6,000 feet, after flying through some light cirrus, we came out into a beautiful clear sky. Below us lay a vast field of cotton wool lit up by the moon. With this visibility it was possible from a good position to see the enemy at 1,000 yards. It was 01.10 hours precisely by the time we reached our combat height of 15,000 feet. Brinos tuned in on the ground-station wave and learned that the head of the British bomber stream was flying west of Nancy on a course south-south-east. In a few moments we should get the first contact in our radar. I circled west of the city and explored the night sky with my SN 2. Brinos reported calmly: "*Achtung.*

BATTLING THE BOMBERS

The first enemy zig-zags have appeared. Turn slightly to port."

The gyro compass showed 160° and changed on a slight left-hand turn to 130°. Brinos now reported: "Target about two and a half miles ahead. Give her full gas."

My C9. ES was very fast. Within a few minutes the distance was reduced to 1,000 yards. At any moment the enemy bomber must appear. I closed in until I could see the black shadow of the bomber. The British machine was flying peacefully, weaving slightly to avoid attack. I recognized the type by its wings: a four-engined Lancaster. Brinos switched off his SN 2 and concentrated on each phase of the ensuing air combat. Slowly we stalked the bomber with the moon behind us. Distance 200 yards. The British pilot must have spotted us for he suddenly did a vertical turn to starboard to give his rear gunner a better chance to fire. I stuck on his tail. The Perspex of the gunner's turret glittered in the moonlight. Just as I got it in the centre of my sights he opened fire with all his guns. The glowworms shaved my machine, but with a slight pressure on the rudder I slipped out of the danger zone. Now I was flying below him and approaching at "elevator" speed. In this way the rear gunner could not fire at me, although the mid-upper gunner was still a danger. This time I would shoot first; of that I was certain. Slowly the long narrow wings rose in the air. As soon as I could see the glowing exhaust pipes I fired between the two engines.

The enemy must have opened fire at the same moment for his tracers hit my wings. I immediately took avoiding action.

"The Tommy's on fire," screamed Brinos into the R.T., nearly deafening me. He was right. Flames were pouring from the trailing edge of the wing. But the crate continued to fly calmly on its way.

Shall I give him another burst I wondered, drawing closer. But the enemy was badly hit and the greedy flames were glowing eerily in the darkness, lighting up the red, white and blue circles. We were now flying close to the enemy, watching what would happen. One of the crew baled out. For the fraction of a second his body gleamed in the light of the flames before he fell into the yawning depths. One after another followed suit and eight men in all baled out. It was high time, for a moment later the port petrol tank exploded and the machine hurtled to the ground, leaving behind it a long fiery tail. I did an aileron turn and watched the grandiose sight of the crashing Lancaster. The comet streaked down to the earth and disappeared through the bank of cloud. A few seconds later a column of flame lit up the night. This was the first kill of the night.

My comrades must have watched it, for a few moments later a second bomber hurtled burning out of the sky. I called my radio operator on the R.T. but received no answer. I dipped my wings as a sign that I wanted to say something, but received no answer. Then I gave a hard kick on the rudder and at last Brinos answered. By his voice I realized that something was wrong. Both he and the gunner were obviously delighted.

"Okay, carry on," said Brinos, immediately switching off.

I was annoyed. I would forbid him officially to cut me off like this and insisted on another reply.

Brinos refused to be disturbed and said calmly: "Carry on, old boy, you're doing fine." Then silence and a belch in the R.T.

They were both drinking brandy! The very idea! All right, my friends, I'll show you . . .

BATTLING THE BOMBERS

I put on full left bank and jerked the stick. I heard a terrific oath and ping! The breaking of glass and the smell of brandy permeated the machine. Well, I suppose I had to be content with this sniff. I righted the machine and pushed the nose well down. The result was that both the gunner and Brinos bumped their heads against the roof.

"That's enough," I heard from behind. So I'd taken the wind out of their sails.

"The rest will follow when we get downstairs," I said curtly and asked for a new course.

The bomber stream was approaching Friedrichshafen. Brinos led me to my next opponent. In the middle of the operation he said: "Don't get so excited, old boy. I've just won the Iron Cross and it must be celebrated. The main thing is that you're on the ball."

I did not reply. A bare twenty minutes later our second bomber fell like a flaming torch into Lake Constance. But now the carpet of bombs was falling on the Zeppelin city. The targets were the Dornier Works, the Zeppelin Company, the Maybach Works and the cog wheel factory. Forty thousand incendiaries and 4,700 H.E. bombs were dropped that night on Friedrichshafen, destroying two-thirds of the city. After completing their work of destruction the formations flew west over Lake Constance towards Switzerland. Once more I glanced at the burning city and the blood red waters of Lake Constance. There was no time to lose. The Tommy was gaining height and was very fast now with his empty bomb bays.

Brinos reported: "Skipper, it's strictly forbidden to fly over Switzerland. The Swiss flak has orders to shoot at any target, whether English, American or German."

"Oh, to Hell," interrupted Mahle, "if the British can do it so can we. Let's make the Swiss a present of a nice fat

BATTLING THE BOMBERS

kill. It will be good for them to learn a little of what war's like."

I let the two go on with their discussion and went on chasing the enemy to the west.

Brinos reported: "Contact directly ahead. The bomber's in a steep dive." Searchlights suddenly went on in the distance. The Tommy made for them.

Slowly I closed in, until I was within 800 yards. The searchlight battery was not far away and in its sheaf of beams I recognized the silhouette of the enemy plane. Another four-engined Lancaster. The searchlights went off but I could still see the Britisher in the dark and approached until his tail was in my sights. At 100 yards our tracers crossed I could hear the bullets rattling on my machine and a little later there was a smell of burning in the cabin. At this point Mahle roared: "We're on fire. The port engine's alight."

As though stung by a tarantula, I raised myself in my seat, broke away instinctively in a dive and closed the fire cock. A burst of full throttle to burn up the last fuel in the lead, ignition off and stationary prop. Nervously I watched the burning engine. Had a British night fighter been in the neighbourhood our last hour would have come. But the bomber must have been pleased to be rid of us. In the midst of this excitement twenty to thirty searchlights went on and we were suddenly lit up as in broad daylight. No orientation was possible. I went into a spin. I stared in terror at the threatening searchlight cone.

"Fire a distress signal, or we shall crash," I shouted to the crew, trying to get my aircraft once more under control. But it was impossible. Not until the searchlight switched off on seeing our signal did I get her once more on an even keel.

BATTLING THE BOMBERS

We had dived 3,000 feet and the electric altimeter showed only 4,500. A pretty business. I cursed those Swiss down below. In the meantime the fire had gone out in the engine, so we were not so unlucky after all. But hardly had I been flying level for a few seconds than the Swiss turned on their searchlights again. Presumably my snow-white machine was a good object for their target practice. Mahle immediately fired more distress signals, for he was terrified that we should crash. We were far too low. The Swiss batteries switched off, fired green flares and lit up the airfield. It was a peremptory order to land, but we did not intend to give up so easily.

We worked according to plan: Mahle fired green flares which meant that we wanted to land. The men below replied with green flares and switched the airfield lights on and off as a sign that they had understood. Now, if only my second engine had been in action! In a breathtaking power dive I should have skimmed over the searchlight battery and flown at tree top level in a northerly direction. With two engines it would have been simple, but my port engine propeller was stationary and I was thankful that my crate was still in the air.

Nevertheless I tried to turn north and get out of the searchlight zone. But the Swiss noticed my turn and switched on so brazenly that I was terrified. This time Mahle fired red flares until the barrel of his pistol was hot, but the Swiss were obstinate. I did my best to keep the machine in level flight but it was too difficult. The glaring cone blinded me and in a few seconds I lost all sense of gravity. Once more we dived and were looking into the sinister eyes of the searchlights.

"Fire red, red, Mahle, or else we've had it."

The machine began to whistle: a gruesome sound. At

BATTLING THE BOMBERS

last the Swiss switched off. For a second I was still blind and then I recognised the illuminated airfield—far behind me. I pulled the machine out before it was too late. I was lucky. The electric altimeter showed a bare 1,000 feet. Now we could not afford to play any more monkey tricks unless we wanted to crash. Once more Mahle shot green and the Swiss replied contentedly with the same signal. I made a wide circle, for to take off again with one engine would have been dangerous. The airfield looked wonderful as the flarepath lights slipped beneath us. The machine sank lower and touched down in a perfect landing near the first white lamp. How marvellous to be on terra firma once more, even though it was Swiss soil. For the moment we were safe. The airfield lights went out as soon as we were down. Ahead of us it was pitch dark and we were still taxiing at 50 m.p.h. into the blue. I switched on my own searchlight and recognised some four-engined bombers ahead: American Boeings. The Flying Fortresses were parked close together. Then the Swiss blinded me with a strong searchlight right in my face. I could see nothing and pressed with all my weight on the brakes so as not to crash into the Boeings. Presumably the Swiss feared that at the last moment I should take off again, but that was impossible with only one engine. Slowly C9. ES came to a standstill.

Suddenly a figure appeared close to me on the wing. I pulled open the cockpit roof and was about to say something when I felt a revolver in my neck. I was dumbfounded.

"You're on Swiss soil," the man on the wing shouted in my ear. "Make no attempt to escape or I shall have to use my weapon."

What a pity, I thought, that my engines are out of action. It would have given me the greatest pleasure to sweep the man and his revolver off the wing by giving her full throttle.

BATTLING THE BOMBERS

But it was no use, so I obeyed. Now we knew where we were—in Zürich-Dubendorf. Somewhat depressed, we got out of the machine. We had quickly stowed our secret documents in our pockets and waited for a favourable opportunity to destroy them. Brinos came face to face with a Swiss soldier with fixed bayonet. He was horrified. "Put that horrible knife away," he said to the conscientious soldier. The man must have had some respect for an officer's cap for he stood at ease and lowered his rifle. Mahle and I could not help laughing and the spell was broken. The Swiss officer, now reassured, put away his revolver and offered us cigarettes.

We were driven to the mess in a Mercedes. A reception seemed to be taking place for, despite the late hour an air hostess in a red evening dress received us and saw to it that we had food, clothes and quarters for the night. The food was magnificent but far too rich for our stomachs which had been ruined by wartime fare. There was a great activity in the next-door rooms. I asked the Swiss officer what was going on.

"Oh, they're your colleagues from the other side who force-landed here during the day. I suppose you heard about today's big raid on the ball-bearing factory at Schweinfurt. The boys left a lot of their tail feathers behind. Over a hundred planes were shot down by the German fighters and nine force-landed here, some with shot-up engines, some with half a tail and others with wounded aboard. Now they're celebrating the end of the war for them. They are to be interned in Switzerland."

This was bitter news to me. Spend the rest of the war in Switzerland? Not on my life. First we must get rid of the secret documents. After the good meal we all felt a sudden urge to visit the lavatory, but the Swiss guard did not leave

BATTLING THE BOMBERS

our sides and stood outside the door, which had to remain open. The three of us sat in the cabins thinking how we could get rid of the documents. It was a long session and the guard began to grow impatient. At a favourable moment I took the papers from my knee pocket and flung them into the pan. A good pull on the chain and they had disappeared for ever. My two comrades must have done likewise for we all left the place looking visibly relieved.

In the meantime the Americans had learned of our presence and greeted us with the greatest cordiality. They slapped us on the back as though we were their best friends and offered us champagne.

"You damned Messerschmitt guys. Why are you fighting for Hitler? Hitler kaput! Germany kaput! Everything kaput!"

We let the Americans go on talking, smoked their Chesterfields and offered them our German cigarettes in exchange. They were rather surprised that we still had anything to smoke and accepted them eagerly, but after the first puffs spat them out and called them stinking weeds. The strong Virginia tobacco made my head swim. I put out my cigarette and refused the offer of others.

"Cigarette no good?" asked one of the captains.

I laughed and replied: "Cigarette good—too good!"

The Yankees laughed uproariously. The Swiss officers were delighted that the pilots of the two warring nations should be on such good terms.

A Swiss Colonel soon appeared to interrogate us. We were taken separately into his office. The interrogation did not last long.

The Colonel asked: "From which airfield did you take off, and what unit do you belong to?"

"Such questions are useless, Colonel," I replied. "You will receive no information from me or my crew. We want to get back to Germany as quickly as possible. Please be good enough to notify our military attaché."

The Colonel had presumably expected this reply, for he gave us permission to retire. From this moment onwards we were not allowed to communicate with each other. The windows of our sleeping cells were barred and a Swiss guard stood outside the door. Thoroughly exhausted I slumped on my bed and was soon fast asleep. Next morning I needed some time to take in my new surroundings. I did not see my crew all day. The necessary formalities were being carried out and we were taken for a further interrogation. The Swiss were polite and correct but I could not help feeling a trifle anxious. The second day passed in endless waiting. My companions knocked on the walls of their respective cells and I devised a plan of escape, for I had no wish to remain in Switzerland. But on the third day of our internment we were taken by train, under close guard, to Berne.

It was an agreeable surprise when we were given rooms in the Hotel Metropole and the uniformed guards were replaced by a civilian called Fuchs. The German General-Consul paid us a visit. We had to get out of our uniforms immediately for in international Berne they might have given rise to unpleasant incidents. Three night fighters in tattered Luftwaffe uniforms were taken to a store and emerged half an hour later as dapper civilians. The German Consul paid for our uniforms and gave us a considerable sum of pocket money. We wandered round the city like harmless Swiss citizens. Everything which had long since disappeared in Germany was to be had in full measure in the shops. Cinemas, cabarets, dance halls and baths were open until late at night. Released from the tension of war and

BATTLING THE BOMBERS

revived by the warm spring air, we enjoyed our liberty to the full.

At this juncture, just as we were beginning to feel really well, our polite custodian Fuchs told us that within the next few days we were going to be exchanged for three Britishers. Three British officers had escaped from a German prison camp in Italy and had asked for asylum in Switzerland. Nothing therefore prevented the exchange of three Germans for three of our enemies. At the end of May, 1944, our convalescence in the golden Swiss cage came to an end. The German military attaché, the General-Consul and a few German families saw us off at the station. As the train steamed out of the station and our friends were waving, Mahle shouted out of the window: "Keep our rooms ready. We shall soon be back." Even the Swiss officers laughed and waved to us.

"Back in the Homeland a new life begins," as the song says. Yes, with air-raid warnings and blacked-out trains in the direction of Berlin. At the frontier 10,000 Swiss cigarettes were handed to me as a present from the German Consul. They would be a boon to the fellows in the squadron. In Berlin the General Officer Commanding was waiting to hear our report. We were still in mufti. The German told us what had happened behind the scenes during our absence. I learned the following:

Hardly nine hours after my forced landing in Zürich, the Gestapo appeared in Homberg, Altenburg and Breslau to interrogate our respective families. A short house search, various photos and letters impounded, the houses closed with an official seal and an hour later our families were under arrest at Gestapo headquarters. Himmler had worked promptly and efficiently. On the same day two men in civilian clothes with diplomatic passports left the capital

BATTLING THE BOMBERS

for Zürich and Berne. One of them had been instructed to blow up my plane and the other to put an end to my earthly existence with a well-aimed bullet. Our families were pestered with questions and squeezed as lemons. As nothing came of the interrogations, the officials grew cynical and locked them up. The food was disgusting; the cells filthy and stinking. There was no water.

The staff of No. 1 Fighter Division soon heard of the events in Berlin. The telephone rang furiously and Goering flew into a rage when he heard of Himmler's actions. The Head of the Secret Police remained unmoved but withdrew the orders for arrest and shooting. The S.S. Führer, who, disguised as a civilian, was to kill me, was stopped by an express telegram at the frontier, but the second man with orders to blow up the machine had already crossed the frontier. On the third day of our internment my C9. ES blew up, under mysterious circumstances, on the airfield of Zürich-Dubendorf. On the seventh day of my internment my family was released, after having given their word in writing that they would never breathe a word of what had happened.

I was dumbfounded when I heard of this. I telephoned home immediately to console my parents. Next day we left Berlin and were flown to Hagenau in Alsace. The whole squadron was out to greet us. It was a happy reunion. When I finally produced the packets of cigarettes and distributed them, the mood was very high in our old Night-Fighter Wing 6. We gossiped late into the night.

I decided to pay a visit to my family in Homberg It was a happy occasion but I found them all very subdued. This sudden arrest and detention in a Gestapo gaol had upset their nerves, particularly since they were not told the reason for their arrest. Neither the Party nor the Government had considered it necessary to apologise for the mistake. Only the General Officer Commanding, Berlin, had expressed his regret for the behaviour of the Gestapo. On my return to Hagenau I took over my old flight. My regular radio operator, Feldwebel Grasshoff, who had been recalled from leave on account of our trip to Switzerland, was delighted to see me back. That same evening we took off to attack the R.A.F. bombers who were raiding Frankfurt.

Chapter XV

MITCHELLS AGAINST US

At the beginning of June, 1944, our transfer to Szombathely in Hungary came like a bolt from the blue. I had never heard the name before, but the German frontiers had changed so radically that we were no longer surprised at hearing Budapest called "a German citadel" and our brothers and sisters in the Batschka referred to as "citizens who have returned to the Great Reich." A fellow pilot maintained that Szombathely was a suburb of Vienna, about half an hour from Grinzing. Moreover, Hungary was the land of golden Tokay, fiery paprika and temperamental Julischkas. What should we be hunting there at night? Although we knew nothing for certain, rumours sprang up like asparagus in spring rain. I gave no thought as to the why and the wherefore and looked forward to this trip to Hungary after my official visit to Switzerland. In Szombathely—Steinamanger in German—we were under the C.O., First Fighter Division, Oberst Handrik. He was just the type of C.O. we liked—a good sportsman, friendly and always on the side of his pilots.

BATTLING THE BOMBERS

He initiated us into our new tasks: the protection of Vienna and Budapest against R.A.F. raids from Italy, and combats with the night-flying partisan aircraft from the east. Whereas in the west the night-fighter arm had been broken up and gone over to free for all—the so-called Wild Boar—we were still flying here according to the old system. Days of waiting passed. There was nothing doing on those warm clear Hungarian nights. Night after night we sat in our huts waiting for the fish to nibble at the bait. The mood of the pilots and the ground staff sank to zero. Some spoke of exile and others of convalescence.

On one of these boring evenings the C.O. brought us a model of the Mitchell, an American aircraft. We looked at this bird from all angles and shrugged our shoulders.

"Yes, that's the crate in which the Russians will soon be paying us a visit," declared the C.O. "The Mitchell is a twin-engined fighter of great quality—fast, easy to handle and heavily armed."

On closer inspection I noticed that it bore a surprising resemblance to our Do. 217, which had recently been put into service as a night fighter. By chance a night-fighter squadron was stationed in Budapest, equipped with these aircraft. The C.O. switched off the light, lit a candle and projected the shadow of the Mitchell on the ceiling. It was exceedingly difficult to distinguish the American from the German. The wings were very much alike, both of them had small bodies and double tail units. Finally the Mitchell had an "engine stagger," in other words the tail of the engines protruded over the wings. This was the only way of distinguishing between friend and foe. The night-fighter C.O. from Budapest had already phoned us up in some anxiety.

"So, gentlemen," said the C.O. bringing his lecture to

BATTLING THE BOMBERS

an end, "be careful of our brothers in the Do. 217s, and don't fire until you're quite sure that you've recognized the type."

The model of the Mitchell was passed round. Oberleutnant Sapp Kraft, an ambitious go-getter, stoutly maintained that any child could distinguish between the two machines.

Another evening of waiting. The sultry summer air made the crews feel lazy. They sat outside in deck chairs listening to a pep-talk speech from Goebbels. In the meantime the veterans exchanged stories of the good old days in the west.

"Yes, those were the days. Here in Hungary our crates are getting rusty."

The hours passed. A storm piled up in the south east; it was probably over Lake Balaton. From hearsay we knew that these summer thunderstorms in Hungary were very dangerous. Shortly before midnight the telephone rang. The Adjutant casually took up the receiver, expecting a pointless conversation, but the crew was on its feet at once as he replied: "Yes, Herr Major. A machine reported, presumably a partisan supply aircraft. One machine to be despatched to Sector Cancer."

The Cancer sector was in the direction of the thunderstorm. Who was to take off? Flying conditions were not good, for the storm clouds reached 24,000 feet with 80 m.p.h. winds. The choice fell on me.

At 00.10 hours I took off with my crew, Oberfeldwebel Mahle and Feldwebel Grasshoff, in the direction of Lake Balaton. I did not have to gain much height, for the reported machine was at 6,000 feet. The pallid moonlight lit up the outlines of the storm clouds. Lightning flashes rent this monster, turning the bank of clouds to an electric blue. I turned away to the west and flew round the bad weather in a wide circle. In this way I had delayed my entrance into the Cancer sector. Finally we were in communication with the ground station. We were given orders to wait and the arrival of another night fighter from Budapest, a Do. 217, was reported. This might turn out to be amusing.

"Well, boys, look out when we spot the enemy," I said to the crew, turning on a course south-west from Lake Balaton.

A good hour passed. The partisan supply aircraft in the meantime must have landed with its weapons, ammunition and radio apparatus and would soon be on the way back. The storm clouds moved further westwards and closed my way to my own airfield. Then the ground station reported the enemy on the return flight. I was given the course and switched on my SN 2.

The ground station warned again: "Do. 217 still in your sector."

"What's the point of this lunacy?" I asked myself and hoped that we should not ram our friends.

Grasshoff had now picked up the target in his radar and was leading me towards it. The enemy was flying at great speed and keeping a straight course. By its behaviour it could be a Russian. At full throttle we closed in . . . 500, 300, 100 . . . and there he was! I dived and bobbed up below the opponent. His wings and body showed up very clearly against the sky. A Mitchell! Swiftly I loaded my guns and prepared for the attack.

At that moment the ground station called again: "Friendly aircraft quite close to you." In great excitement the fight-directing officer called: "*Achung, achtung!* White Thrush from Cancer. Be careful of friend. Do not shoot until you have recognised the enemy."

This fellow down below was making me nervous. Could

BATTLING THE BOMBERS

it be the Do. 217? My wireless operator was also in doubt.

"It's obviously a Do. 217 and not a Mitchell. The Russian wouldn't fly so nonchalantly in this neighbourhood."

I peered out to try and recognize the two staggered engines. I saw them; so it was a Mitchell. My gunner Mahle had not the slightest doubt. "Have a go at him," he shouted.

I was still not quite convinced. Rather than shoot down one of our own night fighters I preferred to forego a kill. What was to be done? I gained height and got in formation position at a respectful distance from the plane. Who knows? The other crew must have spotted me by now. But it did nothing. I switched on my navigating lights—green, red and white—and dipped my wings. It took no notice. Only when I fired three green stars did the other pilot go into a steep right-hand turn and disappear like lightning. Now I knew for certain that it was a Mitchell and streaked after it. But the pursuit was fruitless. The machine was too fast. Neither the ground station nor my sparker picked him up again. What on earth had he thought when I flew in formation with him with my navigating lights on. Possibly he thought that another supply plane was having a little game with him.

Slightly irritated, I made for home. The storm lowered dangerously ahead of me. My only alternative was to land in Budapest, but I did not feel inclined to do this. I therefore decided to fly blind through the broad storm zone. My course led over Lake Balaton in the direction of Tabolca to Szombathely. My altitude of 6,000 feet ruled out any danger of crashing into the Bakony Hills. About six miles from Lake Balaton I entered the gigantic cloud bank. What happened next I shall never forget. In a flash we were swallowed up in pitch-black darkness. The outside temperature sank swiftly to freezing point. The rain lashed against the windscreen and reduced my visibility to nil. From now on I had to rely on my blind-flying instruments: artificial horizon, spirit level, altimeter compass, air-speed indicator and variometer. To have a better view of the instruments I lowered the seat and registered my entrance into the storm cloud on the instrument-panel clock. My crew was now relying upon me, for they could do nothing. The deeper we penetrated the bad weather zone the more the machine was buffeted by the strong wind. Time and time again I had to bring her back on an even keel. Then something happened which I have only once experienced in night flying. It was pitch black around us and the lightning lit up the rain clouds. Then blue lights lashed against the windscreen—slowly at first and then in unbroken sequence. This blue, harsh light outlined the whole machine from the wing tips over the engines to the armour-plated nose. A little blue flame appeared on the points of the aerials and the propeller-blades were clearly outlined with a blue circle of light. We were all terrified. I was so spellbound by this natural phenomenon that I could not take my eyes off the blue lights. The machine shuddered beneath the gusts of wind. I forced myself to watch my instruments, since to stall in this witches' cauldron would mean certain death, but the Saint Elmo's Fire kept catching my eye. My clock registered seven flying minutes, so I must have passed the hub of the storm. Slowly the blue lights vanished. The gusts calmed down and now only the rain lashed the white outlines of my Me. 110.

The radio operator called our airfield and was told that the weather was clear there. Grasshoff switched off his transmission and went on to the beam. The little pointer wobbled systematically from left to right, a sign that we were on the right course. Half an hour later we landed at Szombathely. My pals had naturally been listening in to

BATTLING THE BOMBERS

our conversations during the ops and pulled my leg after I had reported to the C.O. I gave him a completely accurate report and told him of my experience with the Mitchell. Oberleutnant Sapp Kraft shook his head and said woefully that such a thing could never have happened to him. A Mitchell was as easy to distinguish from a Do. 217 as a horse from an ox.

"Probably in daylight, bright boy," I replied.

A few days later I was proved right. On the night of 26th June, 1944, the British attacked the Hungarian capital from Italy. The bombers were already reported over the Adriatic. At 22.45 hours we took off from our airfield. North of Baja, and therefore a long way from the capital, we met the British bomber stream and decimated it. Only a few bombs fell on Budapest causing a few paltry fires. Our wing shot down sixteen of the enemy. During this attack Oberleutnant Sapp Kraft shot down two bombers, a Vickers Wellington and a Mitchell. We were rather surprised: a Mitchell from Italy. It did not seem possible. The thick end of the stick came later. Budapest called and asked whether our fighters had shot down a Do. 217 by mistake. There was an icy silence. The C.O. compared the time of the incident in the operational report with the time of the shooting down of the Do. 217. It could only have been Kraft's Mitchell. The times agreed precisely and also the site of the crash. Fortunately the crew of four managed to escape from the burning machine thus saving him from a court martial. Kraft was depressed. I could not help indulging in a little malicious pleasure and said: "Well, old man, you mistook the ox for a horse." Once more it was a case of he who laughs last laughs loudest.

Nevertheless the success of that night cheered up both

BATTLING THE BOMBERS

the pilots and the ground crews. The crisis was over. We were ready for new deeds.

During the next ops we were to lose one of our best pilots, Oberleutnant Wolfgang Knieling. Knieling, a magnificent night fighter, distinguished himself in particular in the Battle of Berlin. In an air combat over the German capital, he was hit by a flak burst. Badly wounded he landed the heavily damaged machine with his last strength, saving the lives of his wounded wireless operator and gunner. On landing he fainted through loss of blood. The ambulance was quickly on the spot and took him to hospital. After months of his sick bed, he returned to our wing. On his arrival a telegram was waiting for him from home. His young wife had presented him with a daughter. He was thrilled.

The sirens wailed at midnight. A British formation was flying over Croatia in the direction of Vienna. We scrambled for our machines and were airborne within a few minutes. Knieling hobbled to his dispersal pen on his gammy leg. The engines were revved up and in a few minutes the wing was in the air in strength: thirty machines. It was a free for all; each of us flew towards his own destiny. The British skimmed over the Alps in order to escape our radar. At this altitude near the icy peaks I spotted, by chance, a Vickers Wellington. It was thirty minutes after I had taken off. The Tommy must have seen me for he streaked towards the mountains to shake me off. I knew that pursuit would be very dangerous for each moment a rocky wall could loom ahead. But the British pilot gambled everything on one card and went down lower into the valley. On both sides of me the mountains were now higher than my wings. Suddenly a huge column of flame rose ahead of me; the bomber must have crashed straight into a cliff. The flames

BATTLING THE BOMBERS

lit up the neighbouring mountains. At the moment of his impact I zoomed in order to escape a similar fate. The ground station gave me my position: Schneeberg, with a peak of 6,250 feet. This mountain had proved disastrous to the British crew. Strange—a kill without a round of ammunition having been fired.

The pursuit went on. All round me burning machines were hurtling down into this world of ice. The ground station reported once more: "Attack on Sankt Polten in progress. Eight minutes later we picked up a second Vickers Wellington in our radar. The bomber was flying peacefully towards its target and was not far away. The bombs were still in its bays. I attacked immediately and fired with all my guns into the fuselage. The British bomber stream was broken up before it reached Sankt Polten and its bombs fell at random on the city. On the return journey, I had no luck. The Tommies, impressed by their losses, hedge-hopped for home. Oberleutnant Knieling was pursuing one of them. A bitter combat developed above the mountain peaks. Knieling sent his final message: "*Pauke, Pauke!*"

I, too, was watching the exchange of fire, not far ahead. The British pilot replied with tracers. The bursts crossed each other—a short pause and another burst. The Tommy struggled desperately. Knieling gave him no quarter and sprayed him with a rain of fire. Suddenly both machines were on fire. The bomber went down in a power dive and crashed. Knieling remained with his machine on fire for a while in the air, then crashed quite close to his quarry. I circled over the spot, but there was no hope. The burning wreckage lay at 6,000 feet in a world of ice and snow.

After the attack on Sankt Polten, calm reigned in the

BATTLING THE BOMBERS

air by night. Had the losses been too heavy for the Allies or were they preparing a new offensive? The latter must have been true. There was great activity in Warsaw, where the small German garrison was faced with strong forces of Polish partisans. A revolt could break out at any moment but the partisans were in need of weapons and ammunition. But how were they to get them? The overland route was closed and they could only be brought in by air. The British prepared a big air lift from Foggia to Warsaw. Formations of Halifaxes and Lancasters were sent from the British Isles to Italy.

Preparations were under way, but weeks elapsed before the air-lift started. The Luftwaffe Command had known this and transferred some of the crews to the West. I was among them and left on the 17th July, 1944, for St. Trond in Belgium. The flight was from Hungary over Austria and Germany and took two hours and twenty minutes. Here was stationed the night fighter wing commanded by Hauptmann Schnaufer, the ace of the German night-fighter arm. After Oberleutnant Lent, Hauptmann Schnaufer was the second night-fighter pilot to win the Diamonds to his Knight's Cross, just about the time that Lent and his crew were killed in such tragic circumstances.

Schnaufer was considered by the English bomber crews as their worst bogey. At that time they called him "The Spook of St. Trond." Night after night they sent special crews in Mosquitoes to put an end to his activities. Before the British bombers left the British Isles, these Mosquito formations left for St. Trond to sow chaos among the Schnaufer wing by low level attacks on their grounded aircraft. But the stout Swabian always managed to lead the Tommies by the nose. He was always the first to take off and pursue the bombers on their run-in. His crew was in-

BATTLING THE BOMBERS

fected by his youthful energy and courage which had raised the number of kills in No. IV Night-Fighter Group 1 to over 700. His go-getting energy together with great flying skill and cunning led to success which were unsurpassed in the history of the Second World War. Schnaufer never spared himself.

Thus he took off one night alone, when a thick fog had reduced visibility to nil. His audacity paid dividends for he shot down four British bombers. He had a unique success during a raid on Stuttgart. A bomber stream in close formation flew over the Swabian capital. Schnaufer inveigled his way into the stream, sending one bomber after the other into the depths. He was soon up with the leaders.

Just before reaching Stuttgart a machine broke away from the stream. It was the Master of Ceremonies. Schnaufer's wireless operator picked up the machine in his radar. Schnaufer knew that on the success of this combat depended the life of his crew, the life of many of the Stuttgarters and the life of the city itself. He decided to attack but it took him a long time to close in. There was a smile on his face. He knew what he was up against for a Master of Ceremonies was something in the nature of an impregnable fortress. The most carefully chosen gunners sat in these bombers to give their Wing Leader an undisturbed approach flight to the target. The best radio operators watched the air with special radar apparatus. No surprise attack was possible against these crews. Long before the night fighter came out of the dark they had spotted him. They knew his direction speed and altitude within a few seconds. The smallest change of course did not escape the English radar operators who immediately notified the experienced gunners. Schnaufer knew all this but his ambition did not allow him to hesitate. The Tommy must be brought down.

BATTLING THE BOMBERS

His operator kept giving him the distance. The approach went according to plan for the Britisher was cruising peacefully. "Distance 900 . . . 800 . . . 700 yards . . . Aircraft at one altitude directly ahead." Now even our cool-headed Schnaufer was excited. "600 . . . 500 . . . 400. Courier straight ahead."

Schnaufer removed the safety catch and his right thumb was now on the firing-button. He knew that by now the Britisher's guns were probably trained on him. "Distance 300 . . . 200 . . . 150 yards." The operator had hardly given this last report than the crew went nearly crazy with terror. Dazzling flash-bombs lit up the machine as bright as day. A piece of shrapnel went through the cabin and tore the radar out of the wireless operator's hands. Schnaufer reacted as quick as lightning and broke away. This saved his life. The tracers streaked away over the cabin. But the Britisher had shown his teeth. Slowly the pilot ran his hand over his eyes to banish the blindness caused by the flash bombs. His eyes grew accustomed to the darkness once more. The Master of Ceremonies must be still very close and at any second the storm could break again.

"What a bloody business," said Schnaufer into the R.T. "What are we going to do without our radar? Good thing he's flying on a steady course. Perhaps we'll still spot him."

The seconds passed. A slipstream caught his machine and flung it downwards like a scrap of paper. Schnaufer righted her immediately, pushed the throttle full home and suddenly saw his opponent's slender fuselage and broad wings loom out of the darkness. But how should he attack? Schnaufer dived until the outlines of the bomber could be seen only vaguely against the sky. Now he must make the decisive attack from below. He pulled the nose of the

BATTLING THE BOMBERS

machine up and zoomed like an arrow at the bomber. But the latter had been watching and met him once more with a confetti-rain of tracers. The iron nerves and the cool judgment of this Wing Commander came to his aid. He flew for two seconds into the defence fire before he fired his cannon. The Master of Ceremonies exploded in the air, a giant Catherine wheel. Burning fragments fell on Schnaufer's machine setting the starboard engine on fire. He was surrounded by a bright firework display of flash bombs, green, red and yellow rockets and bright parachute flares swaying slowly earthwards. His engine was still on fire. To prevent the worst, he had to close the fire cock and stop the engine. Fortunately no British night fighter was in the vicinity or he would have been doomed. The parachute flares drifted slowly to the ground where the wreckage of the Master of Ceremonies' aircraft was still blazing. The site of the kill was just south-west of Stuttgart.

Schnaufer now found himself in the middle of the bomber stream which was making for the false marker flares. About 400 British bombers dropped their load in open country. A smile appeared on Schnaufer's face. In this welter of bombers a gigantic black shadow suddenly shot above the cockpit of the damaged night fighter. The gunner, who was on the alert, caught the enemy machine in his sights and blazed away with the machine-guns until the barrels were hot. He was successful. The petrol tanks caught fire and the bomber dived earthwards in flames.

"Nice work, Wilhelm," said Schnaufer on the R.T., as he congratulated his stout gunner. "But now we'll take a powder before the night fighters spot us. We can't afford any larks with only one engine."

The Wing Commander put his machine into a steep dive

BATTLING THE BOMBERS

and an hour later the victorious crew landed at St. Trond.

Obituary. Later, as a good Swabian, Schnaufer on a cold February night in 1945 continued his efforts. Taking off from Gütersloh, the Major, who in the meantime had been promoted Group Commodore, and awarded the Diamonds to his Knight's Cross, shot down seven four-engined bombers within ninety minutes. A unique achievement in the history of Germany night fighters. In further bitter combats, he and his crew raised their total of victories to 126.

At the end of the war, the British transported Schnaufer's crack machine to England. The Londoners were able to admire the Me. 110 in Hyde Park. Shaking their heads, they counted the bars representing kills on the tail unit. 124 . . . 126 . . . They would have liked to bring the "Spook of St. Trond" to London but Schnaufer lay in hospital and had no wish to be stared at by the Londoners in Hyde Park.

After the war, he came to a tragic end. To the delight of his mother he took over the family wholesale wine business in his home town, Calw, with the same energy as he had shown during the war. This war pilot who had survived a thousand dangers lost his life on a business trip through France. He was driving his car along a perfectly straight road through a forest when a truck turned out of a side road. Schnaufer used his brakes, skidded and the two vehicles collided. Without regaining consciousness, the ace of the German night fighters in the Second World War died of his injuries far from home.

Chapter XVI

MY OWN COMMAND

I had no luck at St. Trond. Two ops and no kills. But I was soon sent back to Hungary. It had been quiet there during my absence. No particular incidents except the surprising news that our C.O., Poldi Fellerer, had married a pretty Hungarian. We celebrated until late into the night and kept drinking to the health of the young couple. That evening Poldi took me to one side and told me that I was to be given my own command: a squadron that had been increased in strength. The divisional order would be coming through at any moment. It arrived next day. My new squadron was transferred to Novisad near Belgrade. My task: to interfere with the British air-lift from Italy to Warsaw. At the age of twenty-two I had to take full responsibility for all my orders and enforce the regulations. The ground staff went on ahead with the trucks. A Commando prepared our quarters and took care of the technical installations. I took off in formation with twelve night fighters for my new airfield on the 28th July, 1944. We flew low over the blue Lake Balaton and veered off eastwards to the Danube. After crossing the river we turned on a southerly course and now, below us, lay the endless Puszta. Occasionally we roared over a village and the peasants looked up in terror as though a storm had suddenly broken. Although the Puszta is a desert it has its own particular charm, a few small lakes and moors and the endless brown steppe. An occasional, almost biblical well heralded another village.

BATTLING THE BOMBERS

The sun beat down pitilessly on the flat country parching the earth. It was even hot in our cockpits. Towards the south, green fields and extensive cultivations appeared. We flew over the Batschka, a German minority region. Here the villages were larger and more beautiful and the fields better cultivated. Dipping our wings we greeted our landsmen. They waved bright cloths to us and threw their hats in the air. After seventy minutes' flight a small chain of hills appeared on the horizon: the Fruska Gora. Here the Danube bends eastwards towards Rumania. Novisad lies just south of this mountain chain. I made a wide sweep and broke formation. We landed at short intervals and parked our machines in front of the small hangars. My Adjutant Oberleutnant Schulleit, who had been in charge of the Commando, came up with a smile and gave me his report.

Everything was in order. Our quarters were ready and a shed had been cleared for use as a workshop. Mess, headquarters, recreation rooms and huts. . . . Schulleit had organised this in the shortest possible time and satisfied all our demands. The Hungarians were very polite and took a lot of trouble to gratify our wishes. Schulleit was a splendid negotiator. The conversations were in broken German and a terrible mixture of other languages. But even when the Hungarian liaison officer came to an end of his knowledge of German and began to gesticulate in his mother tongue, Schulleit kept saying benignly: *"Igen, Igen,"* as though he had understood. Schulleit was known as "Igen." He had done a good job and late that evening I could report to the Divisional Commander that we were ready for ops.

The July nights in Hungary are very hot. We lay in deckchairs, outside Headquarters at the edge of the airfield, waiting for divisional orders. I assembled the crews and told them of our duties. I took the precaution of detailing

BATTLING THE BOMBERS

two waves to fight the British supply machines. The first wave was to attack them on the flight to Warsaw and the second on the return trip to Foggia. As emergency landing strips we had Budapest, Belgrade and Szombor at our disposal. We had to fly over partisan country. In view of this each crew took a tommy-gun and provisions for three days. Furthermore, on a forced landing in partisan zones, all uniforms had to be destroyed, otherwise there was no chance of the men ever getting back to their own lines alive. The crews made their preparations. My Fighter Controlling Officer, 'Oberfeldwebel Kramer, reported that the runway was ready for landing and, to give stress to his words, proudly turned on the obstacle, boundary and flarepath lights. Everything was improvised and it seemed as though a magician had been at work. I ordered everyone to Headquarters so that we could inspect the airfield with its night illuminations. Kramer gave the necessary orders for starting and landing. There was only one runway, north to south. The east-west axis was not long enough and to take off towards the south was dangerous, for it was in the direction of the small mountain chain. To the north the terrain was perfectly flat. It struck me that the artificial take-off horizon in the west was lacking and I pointed this out to Kramer.

"Hell, Herr Hauptmann, I forgot it. But where can I conjure one up from? We've no cables, no lamps and no poles."

However, Kramer, who in the old days had flown with the Lufthansa, knew how to organise things. In co-operation with Oberleutnant Igen he laid on twenty wooden poles and petrol lamps. The men went out into the fields with spades and axes, planted the poles thirty feet apart and slung the lamps on them. We now had a take-off horizon

BATTLING THE BOMBERS

even though these petrol lamps were rather difficult to see. But it was better than nothing. For the young crews, this artificial horizon was an important accessory on take-off.

That evening we were admiring the glorious starry sky as we had so often done before, when the telephone rang and three machines were ordered to their night-fighting sectors. Presumably an English formation was on the way. Well, that was fine! I grabbed my revolver and hurried to the machine. Mahle and Grasshoff were already aboard fastening their parachutes. With the cockpit roof open I taxied to the start, closed the roof and was the first to take-off for Sector Scorpion. The communication with my controller was okay, but shortly after take-off we received the order: "Return to base." The enemy formation had presumably turned for home. I preferred to think that it was a practice take-off laid on by the division. So I said farewell to my controlling officer Schwartz, who was sitting somewhere in an abandoned nest in the Puszta; he had built up the ground radar station Scorpion with a few soldiers from the Signals Service. I set my course for Novisad and began to lose height. From a long way off I could recognise Kramer's ground lights and beacons. Making a wide sweep I landed a bare twenty minutes after take-off. The mechanics refuelled my machine and I had a chat with Kramer about improving the airfield lighting. The crews stood around watching their fellow pilots land. Oberleutnant Buder, who was fresh to a night-fighting squadron, came in, followed by Feldwebel Hubatsch. Both of them grinned as they reported back from ops and were duly chaffed by their companions. Thirty minutes after landing, Division gave orders for three further machines to take off. The situation was as follows: English bomber formation over the Adriatic. flying a north-easterly course. This time it seemed to be the real thing.

BATTLING THE BOMBERS

I took off once more with Buder and Hubatsch and yet within half an hour we were recalled.

"*Reise, reise, reise.* No aircraft in the air," came over the air.

"Servus, earthworm, sleep well," I said to my fighter controller and landed shortly after midnight on my airfield.

As I entered the mess I met a group of cheerful Hungarian officers. "*Jo estet riwano,*" I heard. "Come and drink with us to international flying good-fellowship." We celebrated until the following morning. Only as the sun rose did I lie down with a thick head on my bed.

The following days were spent settling down in Novisad. Gradually we grew accustomed to the peculiarities of the partisans. At first we noticed the disappearance of the petrol lamps and that the artificial horizon grew even smaller. Kramer cursed to himself, took a tommy-gun and rushed with a few soldiers across the maize fields. In the distance we could hear the sounds of firing. After half an hour the horizon was repaired and Kramer returned.

"Why did you shoot, Kramer?" I asked him.

"Herr Hauptmann, the fellows hide in the maize fields like moles. Do you think I'm going to let myself be shot down by a pack of bloody gypsies? I put the breeze up them, but the next time we'll take some hand grenades. That will make them sit up."

I merely replied, "Igen, igen." That night I took the new crews out on a practice flight. We had been flying barely an hour when the landing machines were fired on from the Fruska Gora. From my headquarters I heard the clatter of a machine-gun and took a bearing. I broke off the practice flight and ordered the machines to be examined. The mechanics found several bullets in the wings and fuselage and, in

BATTLING THE BOMBERS

one case, the main wireless cable was cut. I reflected for a moment what was the best thing to do and took off in another machine to counter-attack. We dived on the enemy positions with all our guns blazing. Silence reigned. There was no firing as we landed. Next evening, however, we were woken by a tremendous explosion. We grabbed our tommy-guns. What was up? Had one of the machines exploded? Fortunately no. As a precautionary measure I had placed a guard with a password on each of them. A soldier reported shortly afterwards that a bridge had been blown up not far from the airfield. These guerilla tactics continued every day. A flak company, felling trees for building their gun positions, was ambushed in a sunken road near the Fruska Gora and murdered. One man got away and reported the fate of his comrades later the same night. Thus there was always some activity, if not in the air, on the ground. It was strange. By day the sun seemed to shine on harmless peasants, busy at their fields and who bowed as we passed. A peaceful sight. But by night hell was let loose and the partisans were in their element.

Exactly fourteen days after my arrival at Novisad we had our first contact with the enemy. Shortly before midnight on the 10th August, 1944, Division reported the approach of a single enemy aircraft from the east. A Russian then! I took off with my crew for sector Scorpion and called the ground station. Leutnant Schwarz reported and said: "Wait." The Russian was still about forty miles away and it would be ten minutes before he could be picked up by our radar. Obviously it would be an aircraft of the type Mitchell B 25 —a rapid, handy machine. The minutes passed. Schwarz led me on an easterly course toward the enemy. The distance soon decreased. Suddenly he ordered: "Left-hand turn to course 260."

BATTLING THE BOMBERS

I pulled my machine round and gave full throttle. My enemy was flying 2,000 yards ahead of me. We should have difficulty in catching him for the Russian was flying at 260 m.p.h. and losing height. Slightly irritated, I gave Leutnant Schwarz a rocket for not having put me on the course earlier. The Russian was already disappearing out of my SN 2. I flew for another few minutes on the same course, making wide circles. Then something happened below. An airfield lit up; it was obviously in the notorious partisan area, for its lights showed a gigantic red Soviet star. A few white lights served to help the pilot land.

I throttled down my engine so as not to make myself conspicuous, for now I must wait until the machine took off again. Half an hour passed. The supply plane, which had brought weapons and munitions, would take back a load of pork and wheat. After an hour, the ground station reported that the Mitchell was on the return flight. The machine gained height and was flying at a speed of only 200 m.p.h. I dived like a hawk from my superior altitude and soon caught him. The Russian had suspected nothing, for he did not imagine there would be any German night fighters in that godforsaken region. I got on his tail and scrutinised the outlines of the Mitchell which showed up clear against the clear sky. I cast a swift glance at my firing control lights. All six of them flashed red. The attack began with a long burst in the left wing which seemed to have little effect. The wing caught fire, but the flames went out after a few seconds. It was now flying slower and I had difficulty in throttling back. His port engine failed. I stalked him cautiously for the crew had now been warned and would sell their lives dearly. For this reason I decided upon a seesaw attack which would give the Russians a difficult target. From a slight superiority in height, I dived on the machine

BATTLING THE BOMBERS

and slipped away through the slip-stream of the Mitchell to port. At that moment I opened the second attack and fired a burst at the enemy's cockpit. The Russian crew replied with a murderous defensive fire, framing me with tracers. Tak-tak-tak ... the bullets hit my aircraft. I looked back at my crew to see that everything was in order.

Grasshoff replied: "Everything okay, Herr Hauptmann."

My second attack was also successful, but the machine did not go down although the left wing was on fire. The Russian gunner was now awaiting me from port. I dived rapidly below him on to his starboard side and attacked again. He had not been expecting this. A few seconds were enough to give him the coup-de-grâce. Bright red flames lit up the dark night. But the machine continued on its easterly course. The rear gunner kept firing long bursts with his four machine-guns. But his aim was inaccurate and the tracers did not find their mark. I could wait and flew away from the burning machine. The crew still had time to save their lives by baling out. At each moment the fire took a greater hold. Pieces flew off from the wings and then the petrol tank exploded, lighting up the red star on the fuselage. With a gigantic tail of fire streaming from its right wing, it dived vertically towards the ground. Involuntarily I dived after him to follow the crash.

At that moment the cool-headed rear gunner must have spotted me. From the doomed aircraft suddenly came a burst of fire which hissed past my wing. I had not expected this. Here was real self-sacrifice. In such a hopeless position the crew should have baled out if they set any value on their lives. But instead of this, they defended themselves desperately to the bitter end. A few seconds later the machine crashed with all its crew. I respected these opponents.

"Crazy fellows," said Mahle, sighing deeply, "and ob-

BATTLING THE BOMBERS

stinate as mules. We gave them plenty of time to save their skins."

Grasshoff called the ground station. Schwarz replied and congratulated us on our first kill in Sector Scorpion. Then he said good night and wished us "happy landings." After two and a half hours I roared over the illuminated airfield of Novisad and dipped my wings. This first success was the beginning of a long series achieved by my squadron. At midday on the following day the telephone rang.

Leutnant Schwarz reported: "Congratulations, Herr Hauptmann, it was a fine show. Perhaps we'll spot another one tonight. You must come hunting in my sector more often."

"Okay," I replied. "Call me in good time so that we can come to grips with the pirates."

But things remained quiet until the 15th August. That night something very curious happened. About 21.30 hours, Leutnant Schwarz reported a single machine flying in from the east—another partisan supply aircraft. I took off a quarter of an hour later and reported about 22.00 hours over sector Scorpion. Schwarz and my radio operator got into communication and the fighter controller immediately gave his first order.

"Wait a little. The enemy is flying in."

Some minutes passed before the second report came.

"Enemy now flying into our sector at 9,000 feet, forty miles away. Go up to 11,000 feet."

I gained height and loaded my guns.

My gunner Mahle reported: "Herr Hauptmann, today the first burst must be a winner. Those fellows get very irritable if we only tickle them up a bit."

"If your guns are sighted properly, my dear Mahle, everything will be all right," I replied icily.

BATTLING THE BOMBERS

Mahle was right. The first attack must succeed or it would be another circus.

"My guns are set at eighty yards," Mahle replied, defending his reputation. "At that distance the trajectories of the four guns meet on the sights."

"Then there'll be no cause for complaint," I replied. After this gratifying retort on the orders from the ground station, I set the machine on an easterly course towards the Russian.

"Distance eight miles. Enemy approaching fast."

Hardly had Schwarz given this order than I saw a bright light between the horizon and the earth. That cannot be a star, I thought. I observed as much to my crew. They all looked ahead and stared spellbound at this white spot which grew larger at every moment. It was, in actual fact, the enemy machine.

"*Achtung, achtung!* Scorpion from White Thrush. Enemy sighted. Enemy flying with navigating lights."

"Victor, victor," replied Scorpion. "Enemy flying directly towards our position, five miles away."

"Victor, victor," I replied. "Pauke, Pauke!"

I banked sharply and got on the tail of the enemy machine. This Russian was really irresponsible! Losing height I soon caught him and flew alongside. It was unbelievable! The fellow was flying with his cockpit fully lit as though it were peacetime. What must the crew be thinking of? I figured it out in this way. In this peaceful sector the Russian would never suspect the presence of a German night fighter. And why should he have done? A few ridiculous partisan supply aircraft were not worth a night-fighter squadron, and the Hungarian flak—they had no respect for that. They were right, for their pathetic batteries would never prove a danger.

BATTLING THE BOMBERS

The machine flew on undisturbed and I could see the pilot at his controls. Without a care in the world I accompanied my "colleague from the other side" and wondered what I should do now. It went against the grain to shoot this sitting target out of the sky.

In the meanwhile the ground station called: "*Achtung, achtung!* You're over our position. We can see him, we can see him. Good hunting."

I should have preferred to let the enemy go, his lighted cockpit disturbed me so much. But my crew pestered me.

"Shoot him down. If we let him through, the partisans will get more tommy-guns and our soldiers will pay the price."

Yes, they were right. He must be brought down, but he must be allowed to defend himself. I looked once more at the pilot's seat and dived away. Then I took aim at the left wing-tip from exactly eighty yards. A short burst from two cannon rang out. They registered a hit. A small fire flickered and went out immediately. They must have been warned. But nothing happened. The enemy pilot banked slightly but did not switch off his lights. I flew close to him and observed that the crew was having an excited discussion. Obviously they were wondering where the shots had come from. I fired another short burst, this time at his right wing-tip. The same thing occurred. A small fire which went out immediately. Now by rights the crew should have baled out for we could not go on much longer with this game. But after a few uncontrolled movements, the machine proceeded on its course. The lights were still on. Now I had to take things seriously or we should have reached partisan country, and there was no point in letting the Russians bale out merely to increase their numbers. After these two warning shots in the wings, I could not hesitate any longer

"Shoot them in the petrol tanks, the gentlemen will be

more comfortable baling out," Grasshoff shouted angrily over the R.T. But I was sorry for the crew and I fired so that if the machine crashed the crew would be able to be saved. I flew close to my enemy. Hungry flames were already licking the starboard tank and lighting up my own machine. At last a man baled out. I began to count: "One . . . two . . .", but the "two" stuck in my throat, for no one followed him. The machine stayed in the air for another few seconds and then went into a vertical dive.

The mystery was cleared up the next day. I learned from Schwarz that the pilot who had baled out, a Russian colonel, had been taken with a broken leg to Szombor hospital. I drove over to see him. The doctor gave me the first report. The Russian colonel had been given orders to fly a group of young cadets over the partisan route. To their surprise they had been hit by flak. When the machine caught fire, the colonel was the only one who was able to bale out. I asked the doctor if I could speak to the colonel, and he gave me permission. I had a strange feeling as I opened the door of the ward. The Russian lay in bed staring into space and hardly vouchsafed me a look. I went over to him, laid a packet of cigars on his night table and shook his hand. He suddenly turned round, smiled and thanked me in broken German for my attention. His face seemed to say: "What is the reason for this friendly visit from a German officer?" Before I explained I heard his account of the previous night's incident through an interpreter.

The crew really had thought that they had been hit by Hungarian flak and had therefore not taken things seriously until the decisive moment came which the colonel related as follows: "I was rather excited by the hits on my wing-tips and looked at the terrified faces of my cadets. The youngsters had no parachutes. So far we had carried out our

BATTLING THE BOMBERS

flights without enemy attack and parachutes are rare in Russia. I had difficulty in calming them. But they had a presentiment of the disaster and stared out into the darkness at the earth which lay thousands of feet below. I shall never forget the questioning look of the youngest, a fair-haired boy of hardly eighteen who sat next to me in the cockpit. When another explosion made the machine shudder and the bright flames from the right wing dazzled us, he grabbed my thigh and stared at me in terror. But once more we were lucky. The fire went out and both engines were still running smoothly. I thought that the worst was over and wanted to light a cigar to encourage the youngsters. No more sign of the flak. My young neighbour breathed with relief and lit my cigar. At that moment there was a terrible crash. One of the boys shouted, 'Fire—the starboard petrol tank's alight.' What happened next was really a matter of seconds. Panic broke out on board. Some of them clawed the floor. I was almost crazy watching this tragedy and could hardly bear to abandon the machine. Then the flames licked the cabin and the acrid smoke enveloped us. The air was searing hot and the light went out. We flew on like this for a while until the starboard engine fell out of the burning wing; the machine immediately dived earthwards. With my last remaining strength I managed to get out of the burning hulk and only came to my senses when I landed heavily on the ground with my parachute." The colonel at these words looked at the plaster on his right leg and went on: "Yes, with parachutes we should all have been alive, for we had plenty of time." "Yes, you had time," I replied, "but do you know why?" The colonel shook his head. With the aid of the interpreter I let him know that it was I who had shot him down and not the Hungarian flak. I had given him and his crew plenty of opportunity to bale out by merely firing at his wing-tips. The colonel understood. Tears ran down his cheeks. Now he could explain the riddle of the flak shots. He looked at me sadly and seemed to say: "You meant well, comrade." Suddenly he took my hand and pressed it. I was embarrassed and left the sick-room without a word. In the town I bought a bunch of flowers and gave a small Hungarian girl a pengö to deliver them to the Russian colonel in hospital.

Chapter XVII

STATION HAYRICK

On the 21st August, 1944, six days after my meeting with the Russian colonel, I shot down my third Mitchell with its Russian crew after a bitter air combat. The Russian defended himself desperately, but my superior firing power finally turned the scales. After this, the partisans gave up their flights, but on the following night the British resumed their air lift to Warsaw.

22nd August, 1944. 20.00 hours. Division reported British bombers flying over the Adriatic on a north-easterly course. My crews were delighted. At last there would be an opportunity for some action. My kills had fired the ambitions of the younger pilots and I had to calm them down as they hovered around, already in full flying kit.

"Take it easy, boys," I said, "and keep your wits about you. Half the battle is to surprise the enemy."

But it was difficult to keep them under control. They followed the path of the bomber stream and when they were

BATTLING THE BOMBERS

reported on the way to Belgrade there were howls of delight. At last we received orders to take off. I took six machines, while six remained in reserve to attack the returning bombers. They flew directly over our air sector. Over the R.T. I gave my crews the last orders and advice. My sector was the most southerly and therefore the leading bombers would enter it first.

The ground station and wireless operator Grasshoff used their radar and the first enemy zig-zags appeared in the cathode tubes. I should have to dive soon to bring the others on to the course. A few minutes after this radar contact, the bulky shadow of a bomber looked out of the darkness—a Halifax. The first attack was successful; flames darted from the petrol tank and the crew immediately baled out. For a while the burning hulk continued to remain aloft, then it nose-dived and exploded on the ground. Once more it was a tragic yet beautiful sight. This was the signal for the general attack. My crews dived like hawks on the bombers, bringing them down one after the other. I counted up to six and then there was a pause. I shot down number seven myself and then followed numbers eight and nine. After three hours the operation was over. I was the first to land and counted the home-coming machines. The pilots behaved like maniacs, streaking across the field and dipping their wings. One after another they proudly reported their kills. Division was already on the line asking for my report. It was short and terse. Six machines engaged, duration of ops three hours, nine enemy bombers shot down without loss. Two machines slightly damaged, the remaining ten ready for further ops. The Division was delighted. Oberst Handrik congratulated me personally on our success. "Well, carry on the good job, boys. They'll be on their way back in four hours. Take a breather and we'll notify you in plenty of

BATTLING THE BOMBERS

time. Good luck." But no one thought of taking a rest. They gossiped about their combats late into the night.

The telephone rang again. The British were on the way back. Now the second wave had a chance of going into action. We received our starting orders at 03.00 hours. Oberleutnant Igen was in the party. I looked at the machines as they took off and crossed my fingers. From headquarters we listened intently for the ground to air communications. After a long wait Feldwebel Hubatsch reported the first contact with the enemy. There were a few anxious moments until he reported again: "*Sieg Heil.* Courier on fire." That was the tenth that night. There were four more to come. I estimated that about thirty British bombers had flown in and fourteen of them had bitten the dust. It was a great success for my squadron, paricularly as all six crews of the second wave returned safe and sound.

During the next few nights we had no peace, for the air lift went on from Italy to Warsaw. The British disregarded their huge losses. Night after night these flying goods trains took the air and night after night we shot them out of the sky. But one of my crew crashed after a tough combat.

On the morning of the 6th September, 1944, I was rudely awakened from my sleep. The N.C.O. on duty stood at my bedside. I rubbed my eyes and stared at him morosely, but he gave me no time to collect my thoughts. "Get up, Herr Hauptmann, get up quick. An American bomber formation reported flying directly for Novisad." I was up in a flash, put on my shirt and trousers and rushed down the steps carrying my tunic. As I ran, the Officer of the Day, Oberleutnant Buder, met me.

"It was high time, Herr Hauptmann. We must get off the field. The bombers are already on the horizon, approaching rapidly."

BATTLING THE BOMBERS

I gave my orders swiftly.

"Oberleutnant Buder, you take care of the machines. Let the ground staff disperse them, put on the camouflage tarpaulins and leave the field at once. The N.C.O. on duty is to wake all the crews. Within five minutes the airfield must be cleared, whether they're in their pants or their pajamas."

"Very good, sir. Within five minutes."

I rushed to headquarters and called up the Division. There was a short delay before I received orders to look for an emergency strip in case our field was put out of action. I replaced the receiver and hurried outside. Mahle and the driver were already in the car with the engine running. My gunner was looking anxiously towards the south. Now I could hear the monotonous drone of the American formation. It had a sinister ring. The sun shone down pitilessly, lighting up the silver birds like bright fish. "Get going for the dispersal pens," I cried. The driver put his foot down and sped to the edge of the runway where the mechanics were putting the last grey-green netting over the snow-white machines before jumping into the waiting truck. It was high time. In a flash the airfield was cleared. Not a soul to be seen on this doomed eyrie. The first marker bombs soon fell. My car stopped and we flung ourselves flat in the nearest ditch. A sinister hiss filled the air, the earth trembled and after a deafening explosion a huge cloud of smoke rose from our sheds. Three waves flew in and after ten minutes our airfield looked like a lunar landscape. The bombers left without any damage to themselves.

The same day I drove off to look for a suitable airfield. It was a long time before I found the right spot. Near Hodschak in the Batschka I found a 700-yard-long meadow broken only by a single ditch. The surrounding country

BATTLING THE BOMBERS

was completely flat, an advantage in the case of a short runway. The Burgomaster of this German-Hungarian village did everything in his power to adapt this primitive airfield to our demands.

The news that night fighters had appeared ran round the village. Within a few moments everyone was on the new field. The village schoolmaster, who was a leading figure, got the villagers working. Everyone strove to level the meadow and fill in the ditch. A large tent was erected to serve as a messroom for the crews. Headquarters was in an empty room at the inn. I did not have to bother about provisions, for the people took it upon themselves to billet all the soldiers. After this successful foray I returned to my Novisad slagheap. Oberleutnant Igen had already organised the loading of the gear. The convoy was ready to set out on the single track railway. The train was already in the siding. The soldiers were eager to hear about their new destination, but no one had heard of Hodschak. The news that they were to be billeted in private houses made everyone very happy.

The machines had not suffered too much from the attack. Only two Me.s were complete write-offs, but two more had to be sent to the workshops. The eight serviceable machines remained with their crews in Novisad. My most important task now was to make our emergency strip ready for ops as regards wireless communication. To this end I sent my Intelligence Officer, Leutnant Löwe, with some men and the apparatus to instal the necessary station. It was a tricky job in that God-forsaken hole. I was extremely surprised when Löwe called me that evening from Hodschak.

"How is it possible, Löwe," I asked, "that you've already

made contact with Novisad? Don't tell me you're also through to Budapest and Vienna?"

"That's not necessary, Herr Hauptmann," he replied. "By the time the planes are ready to take off in Hodschak my communications will be in order."

"But where the hell are you phoning from, then?" I asked.

"From a nice lofty spot. I climbed up a telephone pole and tapped the Vienna line. Before they spot it our conversation will be over. The important thing is that you get a current unit, for the supply here is very inadequate and unreliable. So get hold of a small transmitter so that our crews can find their way back by night to this dreary spot."

"It shall be done, Leutnant. By the way, have you found a name for our station?"

"Naturally. A very simple one. Station Hayrick."

"Well, sleep well in your Station Hayrick."

The following day there was the usual bright sunlight over the Puszta. Not a cloud in the sky. The sun beat down and paralysed all life on the parched earth. The villages were empty. No one stirred unless he were obliged to. In this sweltering heat my crews started in two flights for Hodschak. I went on ahead with the car, for my Me. was not yet airworthy. We drove in the open car and we fixed a tent over our heads to protect us from the burning sun. My crew and the fighter directing officer Oberleutnant Kramer, travelled with me. As a precaution Mahle had brought a sub-machine-gun. But, as I have already said, no one stirred in this heat and the partisans seemed to observe the rule. So we travelled unhindered across endless fields along dusty roads. Mahle suddenly tapped me on the shoulder and pointed upwards. A number of Lightnings were making towards us. I stopped and listened. There was a heavy drone in the air. Then we discovered more

BATTLING THE BOMBERS

American fighters at different altitudes, giving cover to a large bomber formation. I suspected trouble. I hoped to goodness that the fighters had not spotted our machines, which at the moment were hedge-hopping from Novisad to Hodschak! I could not get rid of this presentiment and could hardly wait for our arrivel in the late afternoon. There was great excitement in the village. Oberfähnrich Galinsky rushed up to me.

"Herr Hauptmann, the first flight was shot down by American fighters. They dived out of the sun and took our crews completely by surprise. Ulmer and Hubatsch's crews, on fire, hit a barn. Oberleutnant Buder made a forced landing and only one crew got away. So far we have two dead, two badly wounded and three slightly wounded. Ulmer and Hubatsch are badly wounded. Oberleutnant Buder is all right."

This was a good start. I drove to the hospital where our casualties were being treated by a woman doctor. I gave orders that they should be transferred to Szombor and rushed to the airfield. The local inhabitants were thoroughly dismayed. The attack by the American fighters had taken place directly over the village, just before my pilots landed. Four houses and two barns had been burned to the ground. On our emergency field, thank goodness, there were still five machines undamaged and ready for action. The schoolchildren, with touching care, had thrown maize leaves over the grey camouflage nets so that the machines could not possibly be seen from the air. The same evening the quartermaster arrived at Hodschak station with the goods train I gave the soldiers no rest and made them work until the airfield was in good order and I could report to the Division that I had five machines ready for action Leutnant Löwe had done a good job. Telephonic communication with Vienna and Budapest was functioning as well as ground-to-air contact. The current unit ran at full revs so that we did not have to rely here on the alternating current of the village. The transmitter, too, was functioning. On the first take-off by night everything went well except for a small incident. Our over-eager Oberfeldwebel Kramer had naturally illuminated various obstacles, among others a telephone pole which stood at the edge of the field next to the railway line. I squatted with my crew in a tent lit by a petrol lamp and gave the take-off and landing orders when outside I heard a long whistle. We looked out and saw a train held by the red signals. Kramer tore his hair and rushed out to tell the engine driver the reasons for our red lamp.

On the following day, in the presence of the whole village, we buried our fallen comrades. A mountain of flowers and wreaths adorned the graves of these young men who had met their deaths in so tragic a manner. Mothers and wives whose own sons and husbands were at war wept for the dead as if they had been their own. I made a short speech, for I had known them too well to express in words what their loss meant to me. While the coffins were being lowered into the grave I wondered whether I could have avoided this misfortune. Perhaps it would have been better to have despatched the machines in the late evening, but in war can one ever foresee all the moments of danger? Danger crops up and no one knows when it will be his turn. Deep in thought I left the cemetery and made a balance sheet of my experiences as a night fighter. It began in 1941. In the very first month my pals, von Campe, Redlich and Geiger were killed. And the chain was never broken. I had to be thankful that I was still alive. This self-preservation urge held good whichever side one was on. We were in a mess and my men quite rightly demanded of me firm behaviour and belief in victory. I felt that the mood of my squadron, particularly at this moment of continuous setbacks, was dependent upon my behaviour. It lay in my hands whether I allowed the unit under my command to become a hopeless rabble or instilled it with enthusiasm for self-sacrifice by my own example. The great confidence the airmen themselves showed in me inspired me to overcome all difficulties. Inwardly I was convinced that the war was lost, but it was my duty to continue on this path to the bitter end with my men. This was no blind obedience but a question of integrity. To conquer with integrity is simple, but to lose with integrity needs great self-control.

A few days after our arrival in Hodschak, Division reported several formations flying in from the south. We squatted in our tents and debated the position. Now we could clearly hear the rumble of the front-line guns. The Russians were advancing steadily towards the Danube. Two machines were ordered to take off. It was understandable that I should be in one of them. I ordered Oberleutnant Buder to take off in the second. At 22.31 hours we left our emergency field. As I yanked the machine off the ground I found that I had only just had enough room. Landing would be even more difficult. While I was still climbing the controlling officer sent me after an enemy machine which was flying through our sector at 6,000 feet on a northerly course. At 22.39 I sighted my opponent and attacked immediately. A minute later the Halifax crashed on fire not far from the airfield. This was the only kill that night. In these breakneck conditions I was lucky enough to put my machine down after a bare seventeen minutes' flying time.

On the following days my decimated machines were replaced from Wiener-Neustadt. The crews gradually grew

BATTLING THE BOMBERS

accustomed to the small field and enjoyed the extraordinary hospitality of the German minority. After years of war rations, the Hungarian food had the effect of yeast. I could feel it in my own belly. The female element in the village was extremely generous in all respects and I was soon afraid that my men would be throughly spoilt. Even my quartermaster sergeant put on weight. He was thinking of the coming lean years and filled every possible pot with dripping and goose fat. Within a few days a great friendship had sprung up between the population and the soldiers. The villagers counted our machines on take-off and waited up to count them on their return. I had to report each night to my billet, otherwise my good hosts could not sleep. I slipped each morning about four o'clock into their bedroom and wished them *"jo estet rivano"*. *"Edes anja,"* came the smiling reply. "Now you're all right."

From Hodschak we check-mated the Britishers. Night after night we shot down their bombers and brought their Warsaw airlift to a standstill. On the 22nd September, 1944, these flights ceased. A few peaceful weeks followed, until the Russians were thirty miles from the village. When it became known that we were to retire to Oceny on the other side of the Danube there was almost a panic in the village. The people could not and would not grasp that they had to leave their homes or stay and face a gruesome fate. At the last moment they grabbed together a few essentials, inspanned their carts, wrapped their children up in blankets and set out on the great trek. Everything that they had built up with such industry now had to be left behind. Nearly every family possessed its own big farm with rich fields and cattle. They had grown to be at one with their property, as only peasants who have done all the work with their own hands can be. Despite their distance from

BATTLING THE BOMBERS

Germany these men remained true to their country. They insisted upon preserving their mother tongue. In the school, German was learned as the basic speech and they seldom mingled with the Hungarian population. But now the end was near, an end which entailed little but misery, suffering, self-sacrifice and pain. The women, most of whose men were in the field, had to leave their homes, their farms which had taken a great place in their hearts and on which they had lived happily for so long.

The approaching Russian steamroller forced these men to leave their homes. What happened here was comparable with the great migrations of early days. I cannot describe the terror and suffering of these wretched people. Even tough soldiers cannot bear to see the weeping of women or to hear the wailing of children. The soldiers gave them all the help they could, but many of the women were so terror-stricken that they seemed rooted to the ground. My men harnessed the horses and helped them put their belongings on the carts. When at midday on the 19th October, about two hours before the entrance of the Russian troops, we left Hodschak in our planes the village was almost dead. A handful of people who could not bear to leave their homes, placed their hopes in the humanity of the Red Army!

Chapter XVIII

ACHTUNG! MOSQUITO!

As a result of the Russian advance, we left Oceny for Vat near Steinamanger and withdrew from there to Wiener-

BATTLING THE BOMBERS

Neustadt. On a scramble from this airfield one of my flight leaders, Oberleutnant Supanz, flew into the propeller stream of a landing Do. 217 and crashed into the ground from 150 feet. The crew of three was killed. When I arrived on the scene of the crash nothing remained but a smoking heap of debris. The crew were burned beyond recognition. After the funeral orders came through that we were to retire to Leipheim on the Danube.

Since we had been in Hungary the Allies had bombed the German cities without respite. We night fighters were powerless against this massed attack. The British already had their long-distance night fighters stationed in France and Belgium. Whereas the bomber stream started as before from England, the controlling officers despatched fast Mosquitoes from the mainland to join it and take over the task of aircover. The Mosquitoes lived up to their name. They were the night fighters' greatest plague and wreaked havoc among the German crews. The radar equipment of this wooden aircraft surpassed anything that had previously been seen. It was technically so perfect that at a distance of five miles they could pick the German night fighters out of the bomber stream like currants out of a cake. They were 140 m.p.h. faster than our aircraft, but in addition to this, we were fighting against enormous odds. Against a formation of 600 to 800 four-engined bombers and 150 to 200 long-range night fighters (Mosquitoes) we could put into the air 60 to 80 night fighters which rarely managed to penetrate the stream. It was incredibly difficult to get a bomber in our sights for the Mosquitoes sought us out and sped like rockets to the aid of the bomber. Not only had we the enemy in front of us but also in our backs. All this was a great strain on the German crews. The losses rose so appallingly that science eventually had to come to our aid. It came at last in the form of the Naxos apparatus.

This radar with antennae mounted on the tail of the aircraft warned the night fighter by acoustic signals in his headphones and a flicker in the cathode tubes of the presence of an enemy fighter to stern. When the pursuer was 500 yards away there was a slight ticking in the headphones, the first warning signal. If the enemy closed in to within firing range Morse dashes echoed and the Naxos apparatus shone brightly. It was now high time to shake off the Mosquito with an elegant avoiding action before it stung one to death. The Mosquitoes not only pursued us in the bomber stream but, as a result of their enormous fuel capacity and flight endurance, waited for us as we took off from our airfields. They attacked us throughout the whole operation and interfered with our landing. It was almost a daily occurrence that shortly before divisional ops several Mosquitoes would fly over the airfields and shoot down the Me.s as they took off.

In addition to the enemy's air superiority, we now began to have the greatest difficulties in supply. Fuel was stored in great quantities in the depots but as a result of constant attacks on bridges, roads and railway lines, it no longer reached the airfields. We often pumped the remaining fuel out of several machines to get at least one in the air. This round-the-clock bombing also sowed dissension among our leaders. During the heavy British raids on Pforzheim and Dresden, I received no orders from my wing to take off. On the night of the destruction of Dresden, the 13th February, 1945, the enemy bombers droned at low altitude over our heads but we were in reserve and did not dare to go up. We "little lights" could not understand this strategy.

With the attacks on Pforzheim and Dresden, the Allies

BATTLING THE BOMBERS

mad-dog rage for destruction reached its peak. Just as in antiquity the city of Pompeii was destroyed by the sudden eruption of Vesuvius, shortly before the end of the war, the Allies annihilated the cities which had so far been spared, with a burning rain of incendiaries. In particular the cities of Pforzheim, Dresden and Würzburg.

Pforzheim on the 23rd February, 1945, was the first of these Pompeiis. The city was laid in ruins and ashes and about 17,600 people met their deaths in a hurricane of fire and explosions. During the attack the fire fighters were powerless, but even after the raid the fires could not be put out since the water mains had been damaged and the walls lay ten feet high in the streets. This storm of fire reached its peak after ten minutes. It was so powerful that the rain of ashes was carried as far as Stuttgart and the sky turned blood-red over a radius of fifty miles. On account of the raging flames and the explosion of delayed-action bombs after the attack, the inhabitants dared not leave their cellars and were suffocated. Any who dared to come out collapsed in the white heat of the huge fires. Thousands of blackened and mutilated corpses lay among the ruins.

Even more appalling was the attack on Dresden. Since the beginning of the year thousands of civilians, soldiers from the fleeing armies and refugees from the East had congregated there. The city was full to capacity. On the 13th February, about 23.00 hours, the bomber formations appeared over the city and enveloped it in a single sea of flames by dropping phosphorus bombs. Hundreds remained stuck in the melting asphalt and were burnt alive like flaming torches. Hundreds jumped with their clothes on fire into the icy waters of the Elbe or into the nine-foot-deep water basins from which they could not clamber out. Those who could swim were dragged down into the depths by

BATTLING THE BOMBERS

non-swimmers. The Exhibition grounds in the Dresden gardens were filled with refugees who had taken cover there when the sirens wailed. But even the lawns with their centuries old trees were sprayed with bombs and phosphorus canisters until a forest fire was raging. The burning city was again subjected at two o'clock in the morning with a second carpet of bombs which transformed the centre of the city into a ruined wilderness. The casualties that night are estimated at over 100,000. Most of the bodies could no longer be identified. The human remains were placed on huge steel platforms, sprinkled with petrol and burnt in the open air.

In this frenzied assault against the German army and the German cities, Würzburg had been spared—until March 1945—the fury of a modern war. It almost seemed that this would continue, although for some weeks single British bombers had flown over the city. In the early days of March the foreign news service, citing the famous Würzburg Mozart Festivals gave the news—"*Achtung*, friends of Mozart. On the 16th March we shall play you a Mozart symphony."

An appalling nervous tension took hold of the population, which with increasing anxiety followed the daily reports of the bomber formations starting from England. On the 16th March two large formations started from the outskirts of London; one of them flew to the Ruhr and the other over Northern Belgium, the Eifel and Pfalz towards Southern Germany.

On this night which was to prove fatal for the city of Würzburg I had been in readiness with my wing from 19.00 hours. We still did not know which German city was to be rotted out within the next few hours. Division merely said that two large formations had started from the London area. I got ready with my crew for a tough op. The Naxos

BATTLING THE BOMBERS

apparatus—our talisman against the Mosquitoes—was checked once more, for our lives depended upon it. Half an hour later the fighter-directing officer fired a green flare. Orders to take off . . . Both my engines started well, but then the props stopped. I pressed once more on the starter and revved up. I had injected a highly explosive mixture into the pistons but the engines would not fire. My fellow pilots were already on the runway. I tried once more but in vain. The mechanics rushed up. Feldwebel Schoppke and Obergerfreiter Quandt knew my machine backwards. It could only be some trifling hitch, for these two trusty mechanics had kept my machines in perfect order since my first ops in 1941. I had never had any engine trouble.

"Come on, Schoppke, get in the crate and try your luck," I shouted above the din.

At that moment a young N.C.O. came rushing over from the ops room. "Latest enemy position, Herr Hauptmann. The bomber stream is just short of Ulm. In a few minutes it will be overhead. Probable target Nuremberg."

Hell, I thought. I must get in the air or else I shall be a laggard. Schoppke went on trying to get the engine to run. The last warning came from the ops room over the loudspeaker.

"*Achtung, achtung!* Enemy bombers will be overhead in a few minutes. All lights out. Immediate action stations. Mosquito attacks are to be expected. Careful on taking off."

With or without care I had to get in the air. At last the engine started and long white flames poured from the exhaust pipes. Schoppke pushed the throttle forward and the machine bucked. No sparking plugs failure and no jerks in the engine. I jumped on the wing and slapped my leading mechanic on the shoulder. He helped me to fasten the parachute and I taxied to the start.

BATTLING THE BOMBERS

Grasshof called up Headquarters which answered immediately: "Lobster from Thrush 1—I'm taxi-ing to the flarepath. Please light up when I give full throttle. Switch off as soon as I'm airborne."

"Victor, victor," replied Lobster. "Look out for Mosquitoes. Good luck."

I taxied in the dark and took up my place on the runway. After a brief glance at the instruments and the engines I gave her full throttle. The flarepath lights went on and were switched off as soon as I was airborne.

I had hardly levelled out the machine when Mahle shouted: "Look out, Mosquito!"

I thought as much. The Tommies had waited until the fish was on the line. But I did not intend to make things easy for them. I hedge-hopped over the fields and shook off my pursuer. The British were very tough but they did not propose to indulge in any near the ground aerobatics. My crew breathed with relief. We'd made it. We all felt rather uncomfortable after this display of stunting. I zoomed and forced the engine to take me up to 12,000 feet. On the tactical waves we heard new enemy reports. Suddenly there was decisive news.

"*Achtung, achtung!* Bombers are flying in the direction of Nuremberg. A moderate-sized formation reported over Ulm making for Würzburg. Probably objectives, Nuremberg and Würzburg."

"They're not even going to respect the hospital city of Würzburg," growled Mahle. "There really aren't any armament factories there."

I thought for a moment. Würzburg or Nuremberg. I decided for the former and changed on to a northerly course. The night was reasonably clear apart from a few "regulation clouds" at 9,000 feet. "We might be able to use them if a

BATTLING THE BOMBERS

Mosquito gets on our tail," said Mahle. The air seemed empty. In the distance we saw the ribbon of the Main. The moon treacherously lit up the great river. Grasshof reported contacts on his radar. Then the storm broke. We were approaching the bombers. Before we had got to the enemy, the Master of Ceremonies had dropped his marker flares over the city. Parachute flares drifted slowly down, making the night look ghostly.

"Courier 800 yards ahead," reported Grasshof.

At that moment a slight ticking began in my headphones. Long-range night fighters! Despite this warning I remained on my course and gave my Me. full throttle. The ticking grew louder.

"Mosquitoes," shouted Mahle.

I took avoiding action. The British pilot's tracers went wide below my right wing. The hunt started again. Now we were flying directly over the city among the bomber stream.

Then the appalling destruction began. On the orders of the Master of Ceremonies the four-engined bomber crews opened their bays and rained incendiaries on to the city below. The phosphorus ignited as soon as it hit the air and joined into a huge burning cloud which slowly settled on the city. It was a Dantesque and terrible sight. Those unfortunate people who were still in the city! This fiery cloud knew no pity. It sank on churches and houses, palaces and citadels, broad avenues and narrow streets. At the outset burning drops spurted from the cloud causing isolated fires. Then the burning veil enveloped Würzburg. In a few moments a gigantic patch of flame lit up the dark night and turned the clouds to scarlet. Würzburg was burning. By the glow of the doomed city the bombers found their direction. The small wings and slender bodies gleamed bright-

BATTLING THE BOMBERS

ly. I could have shot time and time again, but as soon as I was in position Mahle shouted: "*Achtung!* Mosquito!" I had instructed him only to warn me in case of great danger. Thus I dared not reflect when his words rang out. The delay of a second and we should fall like a blazing torch out of the sky. Then a four-engined Lancaster crossed my path. Without a thought I poured a long burst into its fuselage and wings. The crate exploded in the air and spun down with its crew. That was my only kill over Würzburg and incidentally my last kill of the war. It attracted the entire enemy night fighter pack on my heels. We could hardly watch the bomber crash on the ground before they set upon us. The Naxos apparatus lit up constantly. Mahle no longer shouted "*Achtung!*" but sat and fired his tracers at the Mosquitoes. No avoiding action—no banking—no hide and seek in the clouds was of any avail. The British pilot remained on my tail. Fortunately he always began from long range and his aim was inaccurate.

And then suddenly Mahle shouted in terror, "Mosquito close behind us."

His voice made me shudder. Even as I banked the burst hit my machine. There was a reek of smoke and fire. Terrifying seconds ahead, but I let my machine dive to be rid of my pursuer. The altimeter fell rapidly—2,500 . . . 2,000 . . . 1,500 . . . 1,000. Now I had to pull out unless I wanted to go straight into the ground. I pulled with all my might on the joystick and got the diving machine under control. Luckily the controls answered. There was still an acrid smell of smoke in the cabin. Perhaps a cable was smouldering, but the engines were running smoothly.

We hedge-hopped over Swabia towards our airfield Leipheim. Mahle lit up the cockpit with his torch. Everything was in order. Then he focused it on the engine. There was a white trickle on the starboard wing. Petrol! One of the pipes had been shot through and the fuel was leaking out. The needle on the fuel indicator slowly sank to empty. This was a fatal situation. But misfortunes never come singly. Mahle reported reactions in the Naxos, and the sinister tick-ticking started again in the headphones. The British never give up. This one pursued us even to our airfield. We had to land and avoiding action was impossible. It was pointless coming down anywhere except in Leipheim. Grasshof called the airfield which replied faintly. A few terrifying minutes . . . I pumped the petrol from the port into the starboard tank with the electric pump. Would we have enough? If the right engine conked it would be the end. I now spoke to the ground station myself. Everything depended upon a skilful landing or else the Mosquito would shoot me down as I approached the runway.

"Lobster from Thrush 1. Come in, please."

"Thrush 1 from Lobster. Victor, victor. Loud and clear. Take care—night fighters circling the airfield."

That was to have been expected. The Britisher did not want to miss me.

I replied, "Victor, victor. I must land. Little fuel left. Don't light up. I'll land blind. Put a white lamp on the landing cross and one red lamp at the end of the flarepath. Don't switch on."

The ground station had understood my plan to fool the Mosquito. Mahle sat at his guns in the rear cockpit. I lowered the wing flaps to 20° and circled at low speed over the airfield. The British were searching. The ticking in my headphones was continuous, but the fellows did not dare to come down. I was more than 100 feet above the ground. Tensely I watched the proceedings on the runway. At any moment the two ground lights would go on. The perspiration was pouring from my forehead. I only hoped that the two lights would be sufficient to bring my machine down in safety. I must rely entirely upon my instruments, for the two petrol lamps would neither give me my height nor the direction of the machine. Should I not let them turn on the lights just as I landed? But this seemed too risky. The Mosquitoes were looking with Argus eyes at this field, and if it lit up they would immediately see the machines parked and the sheds. During these reflections I gained height. The red control lamps of the petrol tanks lit up. That meant fuel for not more than five minutes. I must land . . .

I had tuned in my radio to the ground station in order to give the Tommies no hint. But now I was in great danger. I pressed the button.

"Lobster from Thrush 1. Hurry please, hurry please. Fuel for another five minutes."

Oberfeldwebel Kramer replied at once. "Thrush 1 from Lobster. Lamps in position. You can land." We looked for them and Mahle was the first to discover them. They gave a very faint light. Directly above the white lamp I started the stopwatch and set my machine on its course. The white light disappeared behind the tail unit. If I flew correctly as I came in over the field it would bob up ahead of me.

Mahle suddenly shouted: "There one ahead to starboard. A bit higher."

I only caught a glimpse of exhaust pipes disappearing in the darkness.

"For God's sake don't shout so loud, Mahle," I replied.

The seconds passed. If only my fuel would last out. A short pressure on the hydraulic gear. Undercarriage lowered . . . At any moment now the white lamp would appear in the darkness. My eyes peered into the night.

BATTLING THE BOMBERS

There it was. Throttle back. Float . . . The wheels touched down. I put on the brakes and the machine gradually came to a standstill. We'd made it. Grasshof opened the cockpit roof.

"Herr Hauptmann, the Tommies are droning right overhead. Something's up."

I cautiously gave a little throttle to prevent the flames darting from the engine. Any reflection would betray us. In the darkness we taxied to our dispersal pen. Then the accident happened. An over-eager mechanic, trying to be helpful, flashed his green torch. The Mosquitoes were on the watch.

I turned the machine into wind and cut off the engine. Mahle shouted: "Put that torch out, you bloody fool." At that moment we heard an increasingly loud whistle in the air. The Tommy was diving on the airfield.

"Quick, get out of the machine. It's going to get hot here."

Too late. The British pilot shot and the tracers made directly for us. Instinctively I ducked and there was a sinister rattle in the machine. I sprang out of my seat on to the left wing and fell over Grasshof and Mahle as I slipped to the ground. A Feldwebel was writhing on the ground. Then the second Mosquito made its attack. The burning machine made an easy target. With a few leaps we got clear of the machine and lay flat on the ground. Grasshof and Mahle were close behind me. The second burst was a winner. Our good Me. 110 exploded and went up in flames. Now the British were in their element. Powerless, we had to watch two more night fighters go up in flames. Our wretched flak began to fire but with no success. Or did they? The Tommies suddenly flew off to the West. Only then did we come to our senses. The fire engine came up and put out the fires. Near my completely burnt-out machine were two soldiers. One of them, an N.C.O. from the fighter control staff was dead and the other badly wounded. By a miracle we were unhurt, apart from a few scratches.

My driver Vacha fetched me and said: "Herr Hauptmann, once more you've got away with it."

Kramer, the fighter controller, flung his arms round my neck. "I have never sweated so much in my life," he said. "The Tommies are getting more and more impertinent."

Feeling quite exhausted I got on the line to Division and gave my report: "Raid on Würzburg, British dropping phosphorus canisters. The city is on fire. Strong fighter defence. A four-engined Lancaster shot down. Further details not observed. Machine shot up on landing by Mosquito. One dead, one wounded, two further machines destroyed."

Chapter XIX

THE LAST ORDER

1st April, 1945. The last flash before the end. The Allies were fighting in the heart of Germany. Everything was collapsing but Goebbels still prophesied final victory. Werewolves operated in the rear of the enemy. The Führer defended the capital.

This period just before final defeat was a great strain on my nerves. It was a most difficult time for the responsible C.O. of a night-fighter wing. What could I say to my troops? How could I keep up their spirits? Was further sacrifice any use? The men understood me. We went the same way together to the bitter end in our old comradeship. There was no more night fighting. My pilots flew night after night independently attacking tanks and columns of trucks. Many did not return. The Americans pressed on to Ulm. We retreated to München-Neubiberg where we joined up with the other remnants of the Luftwaffe—day fighters, night fighters, bombers, recce planes and Stukas. Mysterious machines landed and took off again. Even General Galland appeared. He had fallen into disgrace with the Führer but was very popular with us. In his jet fighter he attacked the bomber stream and shot down several Flying Fortresses.

A little lull for me. I sent a heavy truck to Ingolstadt to pick up a load of splinter bombs for our attacks on enemy columns. The munition dump blew up shortly before the arrival of the truck. The driver came across a fully-stocked supply dump and brought back 100 crates of brandy and tinned food.

20th April, 1945. On the Führer's birthday each soldier was issued with three bottles of brandy, three tins of food and cigarettes. Spirits rose. Major Fritz, an old reservist, reported that my wing was present in full complement. What should I say to them? I gave a flashback to the successes of our No. III Night-Fighter Wing 6 and ended with the words "Comrades, a difficult path lies ahead. A path into an obscure future. We must take this road with a brave heart and in the conviction that one day the sun will shine once more. Preserve the spirit of comradeship in your hearts. Think of our fallen comrades and do not forget the reason they lost their lives. For our Fatherland—for Germany."

A few days later my C.O. from Venlo days, Oberleutnant Streib came into the mess. My thoughts returned to the old No. I Night-Fighter Wing 1—to my dead comrades Frank, Knacke, Lent, Meurer, Strünning, Wandam, Forster, Herzog,

Schmitz and many others. We swapped memories and thought of the great days of night fighting over Holland. They were in the past. That day heavy shadows lay over our country, and the storm clouds had darkened the sun. In the evening we said goodbye and wished each other good luck.

On the 28th April, 1945, the last command came from Division. We retired to Bad Aibling. The American tanks were at the gates of Munich. On the night of the 30th April my No. III Night-Fighter Wing 6 were given their last operation. Shortly after midnight, with a heavy heart, I gave orders for them to blow up the remaining machines.

Fate has dispersed my friends in all directions. But one thing we have all preserved in our hearts: fidelity to flying, wartime comradeship and the proud memory of our night fighting days.

The End

Printed in the USA
CPSIA information can be obtained
at www.ICGtesting.com
CBHW032155171124
17572CB00008B/330